Human Dreaming

Human Dreaming

The Dynamics of Dream Interpretation

Britt Sheflin C.Ht.

Human Dreaming: The Dynamics of Dream Interpretation. Britt Sheflin C.Ht.
ISBN 978-0-6489994-0-9
Copyright © Britt Sheflin. All rights reserved.
First published in Australia by Sunshine Press in 2020
Cover design by James Hickey and Fiverr-Priticreative
Cover photo by Alex Azabache from Pexels
Book design by Connie Berg
Interior graphics by Aurora Alin

For my parents and grandparents, who supported my wildest dreams.

For my siblings, who love fiercely.

For Larry, who brought us together.

For Craig, who shares his dreams with me.

For Tala, who is a dream come true.

Contents

Introduction 1
Chapter 1 The Existential Questions 10
Chapter 2 Life Script 27
Chapter 3 Your Own Expert 35
Chapter 4 Steps 1 & 2: Dream Types & Subtypes 39
Chapter 5 Step 3: Physiological and
  Psychological Aspects 53
Chapter 6 Step 4: Emotions 60
Chapter 7 Step 5: Symbolic and Literal Aspects 65
Chapter 8 Step 6: Keywords and Phrases 71
Chapter 9 Step 7: Visual Overview and Conclusion 77
Chapter 10 Examples and Case Studies 87
Chapter 11 Mental Cinema 141
A Parting Thought 151

Introduction

Dreams are illustrations...from the book your soul is writing about you. – Marsha Norman

Have you ever wondered what it would be like to be able to have access to the wealth of knowledge that is stored in your subconscious mind? Have you ever had an impactful dream and wondered what it was trying to tell you, only to discover that there are countless dream interpretation books that deliver symbology as if it is a one size fits all prospect?

Imagine being able to peer into your subconscious mind with clarity and understanding; consciously deciding what no longer serves you, and then releasing or transforming it. A powerful way to experience this life-changing dialogue is through Dynamic Dream Interpretation. By following 7 easy steps and breaking down your dreams into simple component parts, the significance of each dream becomes clear.

In the first three chapters you will learn:

- What dreams consist of
- Where they come from
- How dreams affect you

Britt Sheflin

Chapters 4 through 9 teach you how to break them down into seven manageable parts:

1. Dream type
2. Dream subtype
3. Psychological and physiological aspects
4. Emotions
5. Symbolic and literal aspects
6. Keywords and phrases
7. Visual overview and conclusion

Chapter 10 contains case studies of actual dream interpretations and what value the dreamer was able to gain from their dreams.

Chapter 11 helps the dreamer take the valuable insight gained from their dreams and use it to create a better understanding of themselves.

As human beings, dreams are the essence of, and the vital force behind, who we are. The various ways in which we dream - and subsequently integrate those dreams into the reality of our existence - is the foundation of every action we take, and every experience we have. To be human is to dream.

In popular western culture, dreams are often written off as a jumble of nonsense, yet they occupy a full one-third of our lives. If you also consider daydreaming, that percentage increases to more than half. When we take the time to understand our dreams, and integrate this dialogue into our daily lives, not only are we harnessing the power of our subconscious to assist with the fulfillment of our conscious desires, but we also may live a more fully aware and appreciated life. Sleep becomes something greater than a large period of time where we simply shut down, it becomes a time of great learning. A time where we gain an entire one-third of our lives back.

So how do we make our sleep time more meaningful? By asking the right questions about these messages from the dream world, by separating the literal from the symbolic, and the physiological from the psychological, so that we are able to create a meaningful dialogue between the conscious and unconscious minds.

Dreams are dynamic and ever changing. A wolf, the ocean, or an airborne zeppelin will mean different things to different people. And what about the emotions behind those symbols? To some a wolf may represent freedom, while to someone else it may represent fear. The ocean may represent tranquility to one person, while it defines emptiness to another. The airborne zeppelin may represent achievement or disaster, depending on your subconscious associations. To understand what your own unique symbology means to you, you need to learn the structure of a new language, and that language is called Subconscious Symbology.

As a child I had a variety of vivid, recurring nightmares. Oftentimes they included sleep paralysis (a common sleep phenomenon, where the mind is awake, and yet the body is unable to move or speak. This is frequently accompanied by a feeling of suffocation, with one or more "entities" sitting on, or gathered all around the sleeper.) Almost nightly my dreams included houses with intricate architecture, hidden rooms, and sometimes empty voids below, that had to be traversed via a rickety and narrow bridge.

Eventually, the scary dreams faded away, but the architecture dreams have stayed with me so consistently that I have a variety of detailed house plans drawn up for an array of landscapes and climates. These dreams (both the good and the bad), absolutely fascinated me. As a young adult, I began writing detailed dream journals, and after many years, became so adept at recalling my dreams in vivid detail, that I was able to write just one or two sentences, or sometimes a simple drawing, that would bring entire dreams flooding back, months and even years later. However, I still didn't know what they meant! Only the most literal of dreams were so easily interpreted as to have any real value in my daily life.

It was during this period of intensive dream journaling that I began having predictive dreams. I would dream something, and then it would happen! With a feeling related to, but distinctly different from déjà vu, I would review my dream journal entries, often to find it was accurately predicted. Being mostly science-minded, with few metaphysical leanings, this was more than I could handle. It caused me to take an extended break from writing down my dreams.

A decade later, I had a freak accident that reignited my passion for dreaming and understanding dreams in a rather roundabout way.

Driving my two-year-old daughter home from preschool one day, I had a strong intuition that even though I had the green light, I should be very, very careful about going through the intersection. I looked left, I looked right. My light was green, theirs was red, and everyone was appropriately stopped at the intersection. The cross walk began to count down. I saw no logical reason to justify skipping my green light, so I went. Suddenly, a large SUV with a bully bar on the front came barreling through the center of the intersection at a high rate of speed. They hit me directly in the driver's side door, as I attempted to swerve. The sound was deafening. The airbags failed to deploy, and my head and left arm went through the driver door window. The impact sent us careening through the intersection and we smashed into a Jeep on the far side of the intersection. We finally came to a stop into the curb, by a highly frequented bus stop (which was fortunately empty). Three near-simultaneous impacts that changed the course of my life (and brought me back to dreams).

During one of those impacts, a rivet that held one of the windshield wipers punctured the front windshield, leaving what looked like a bullet hole, and vaporizing powdered glass into my face, eyes, mouth, throat, and nostrils. I was extracted from the car by good Samaritans, and while waiting for the ambulance I examined my terrified daughter (who was thankfully okay). My disoriented and bloodied self knew that something had fundamentally changed in that moment. My life would take a new turn.

After the accident, I discovered that I had anosmia (a complete loss of the sense of smell and taste) caused by damaged nerves, and powdered windshield glass in my sinuses. This was a big problem, because at the time, I had a dream job as a private chef, working for a tech company in Los Angeles' Little Tokyo. I made International Cuisine, with lots of variety, flavor, and character, for a group of people who were just as diverse as the menu. I'd worked with these people and refined my cooking to their distinct palates over the course of the previous ten years. I felt a sinking feeling of loss for this career that had defined so much of my adulthood, and self-identity, not to mention the pleasures and sensations of delicious food from a beautiful kitchen. I was Chef Sheflin! And suddenly, I wasn't. I would still dream of food, the flavors and aromas drifting through my dreams. My brain remembered, but my body had lost the ability to taste and smell.

I knew I had to make a new plan for my career. I had remembered how blissful giving birth to my daughter had been with self-hypnosis, and during a brief period as an assistant in a Las Vegas hypnosis show, how fascinated and impressed I was with the power of hypnosis. I also love teaching and helping people. So, it quickly became clear what my next chapter was. Coincidentally, I lived near the best hypnotherapy college in the country (and quite possibly, the world). With new ambitions in mind, I applied to Hypnosis Motivation Institute where as a resident, I earned my Certified Hypnotherapist, (or C.Ht.) title and received the prestigious Director's Award. My goal of learning to help others as I had been helped with hypnosis had been achieved.

From the onset of my training I discovered how dreams play a pivotal role in Kappasinian hypnotherapy. Kappasinian hypnotherapy is particularly good at pinpointing the way a person takes in information subconsciously, and tailoring it to their unique needs. It is well known for being able to help those who think they "cannot be hypnotized". I still remember the first dream therapy class I took with Dr. John Kappas' son - George Kappas. It was here that I learned how predictive dreams work, and how they can be explained both scientifically and metaphysically (more on this in chapter 4). I was riveted. I immediately renewed journaling my dreams. I began analyzing their content, and the dreams of anyone who asked. Highlighting the different aspects of dreams. Thus allowing them to find the complete meaning by asking themselves pertinent questions, and a tangible foundation upon which to build a thorough interpretation.

Meanwhile, I was no longer frightened by the content of my dreams, but rather empowered in being able to identify the dream type, and assign meaning to the literal and symbolic aspects. I also felt confident in my ability to help clients, friends, and family discover the power in understanding their dreams.

The intuition I had before our life-changing car accident was the same inner voice that guided me on my way to becoming a hypnotherapist. I was learning how to effectively communicate with my subconscious, that marvelous machine that can predict likely scenarios with incredible accuracy. By deciding to become a Certified Hypnotherapist who utilizes dream therapy with my clients, I had a powerful tool at my disposal. I analyzed thousands of dreams throughout my internship, and consequently was able to help nearly as many people gain greater insight into their subconscious messaging.

After countless requests for dream interpretation, I decided to write this book. I want you, the reader, to create a more meaningful life by becoming an expert on your own subconscious, a master of your inner domain.

In the following chapters, you will learn:

- What dreams are and why they are important
- How to break your dream down into seven components:
    - Dream type
    - Dream subtype
    - Psychological/physiological
    - Emotional content
    - Literal/symbolic aspects
    - Keywords and phrases
    - Visual overview and conclusion
- How to use the seven components to understand the meaning of your dreams
- How to decipher your own unique Subconscious Symbology
- How to create a dialogue with your subconscious mind
- Learn what the difference is between a dream, an aspiration, and a fantasy
- Why the emotions of a dream are as important as the symbols
- How to apply Dynamic Dream Interpretation to your daily life, for greater understanding, control, and fulfillment

This book is intended to help you become your own expert on interpreting your dreams. It cannot make you an expert on other people's dreams. However, clinical psychotherapists and hypnotherapists may want to utilize these techniques to help facilitate their client's dream interpretations to learn more about subconscious blockages that may be preventing the client from moving forward. It's fine to be a casual facilitator, helping friends and family learn how to interpret their own dreams, so long as the dreamer remains the expert on the final meaning of the dream.

Dynamic Dream Interpretation is intended to be done by the dreamer, for the dreamer - because the dreamer is the only true expert on their own life experiences. By understanding our own subconscious mind, we begin to comprehend information that wouldn't otherwise make sense. Dynamic Dream Interpretation alone can help the dreamer move forward through greater understanding of their subconscious motivations. Even faster growth may occur when you present your recent dream interpretations to a skilled dream therapy practitioner.

Are you ready to learn what your dreams are telling you?

Britt Sheflin

Chapter 1 — The Existential Questions

Dreams don't come true, they are true.
— *Tom Robbins*

Human Dreaming, Human Doing, Human Being

What are dreams, and why are they important? When we dream, we build the pathway for doing. By doing, we acknowledge our being. By simply being, we open the door to dreaming. It is through this cycle that we create doorways to new realities. So, as a human being, you are also a human dreaming, and human doing.

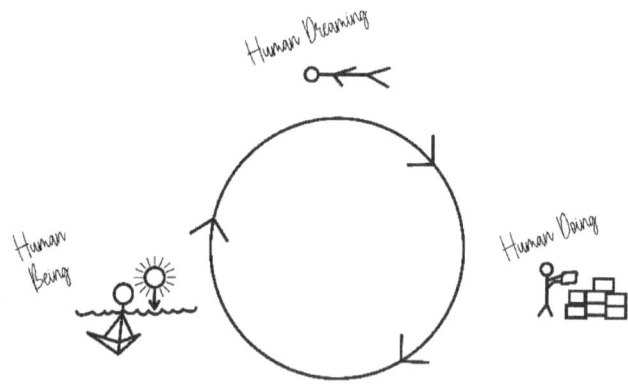

Human Dreaming

Dreams pass into the reality of action. From the actions stems the dream again; this interdependence produces the highest form of living. – Anais Nin

Dreams are important because they directly affect our reality. So how do we know what they mean? How do we utilize them to maximize our own potential? By asking the right questions.

In the following chapters you will learn a step-by-step system for breaking down your dreams into various aspects. Asking all the right questions allows you to decipher your dreams with accuracy and greater understanding than ever before. Additionally, you may choose to learn techniques that help you communicate back to the dream world and subconscious mind by creating an enhanced dialogue between the conscious and unconscious.

Change occurs only when the conscious and subconscious minds are in alignment. If you've ever tried to quit smoking, lose weight, or change a bad habit, then you know that willpower alone doesn't cut it. Systemic changes to your subconscious associations are what allow your conscious mind (willpower) to activate. Perhaps you finally found the right program or therapist, or maybe a health scare prompted your subconscious associations to change. Perhaps there was another reason, but one thing is certain, getting your subconscious motivations in line with your conscious desires is what allows the necessary actions to take place.

Psychologists, Neurologists, and Hypnotherapists often state that our conscious minds (logic, reasoning, and willpower) account for about 5-10% of our daily actions and decision making, and that 90-95% of our lives are being dictated by the subconscious, or unconscious mind. Your subconscious mind is exceedingly good at storing away information that serves to protect you from danger. Remembering patterns of what to look out for allows you to think with your conscious mind, while simultaneously running background programs like: putting your shirt on, tying your shoes, or driving that familiar route.

The subconscious mind is a learning machine that filters and processes information at an astounding rate, one that our conscious minds couldn't possibly keep up with. It stores a wealth of knowledge accessible to us, so long as we learn how to access it.

Knowing exactly how much information our brains store is challenging since our brains store information in a unique way. However, if we were to imagine our brains as having the storage capacity of a computer, estimates indicate that our brains would retain over two million gigabytes of data. But unlike a computer memory with its 1's and 0's, the mind files away this information in the forms of images, symbols, sensations, and emotions. It is these components that make up our dreams, and we can learn so much from them, once we learn how to decipher our own unique hieroglyphics.

Dreams are one of the most important gifts bestowed upon humans. We are avid puzzle solvers, and most of the obstacles we aim to remove revolve around how we want to be or exist in this life. Everything we have created, from pyramids to airplanes, was first a dream, then a plan, and then a reality. When we present our conscious mind with a challenge, our subconscious mind dutifully takes on the enormous task of sorting through all the details. This occurs both day and night, while sleeping and awake. When the task is complete, often when we are in a state of relaxation, sometimes hours, days, weeks, or months later, it presents an exciting image, thought, or idea.

Sometimes these newly formed concepts come in the form of a daydream or a sleeping dream. Sometimes, we do not quite understand the messages or symbols the subconscious mind is presenting to us, even as we feel their intensity. But we can learn! By asking the right questions of our human dreaming parts, we can tease out more meaning, more answers, and more understanding for our human being and human doing parts.

Conscious and Subconscious

You will frequently see me use unconscious and subconscious interchangeably. The conscious mind often likes to create change, while the subconscious (or unconscious) mind prefers homeostasis. Homeostasis is the strong drive to maintain an emotional "comfort zone" and is a protective mechanism. It is hard to create change in our lives when our subconscious controls 90-95% of our actions and has a tendency to get us to stay in safe, protected, and familiar surroundings. How do we embrace that change, while still allowing the unconscious mind to do its job of protecting us from harm?

By creating a dialogue between both the subconscious and conscious.

Through understanding the deeper meaning of dreams, we are able to release unwanted thoughts, feelings, and behaviors, and replace them with new, healthier ones. We are proactively taking the reins and steering our perception of life in the direction of our choice. In other words, our conscious desires are more easily realized when the subconscious mind is in agreement with our decision-making mind.

When our dreams and ideas feel like insurmountable obstacles instead of exciting pursuits, it is often because we have the opposing forces at play. Desire for homeostasis (safety and comfort in what is already known) versus the innate desire for change and growth (risk, reward, and the unknown). We need both aspects or we would be too unadaptable, either by remaining stuck in our childhood programming; or too reckless if we associate risk as the only pleasure. The key to safer growth and change is getting the conscious mind to decide what risks are worth taking, and then getting the subconscious mind on board with taking the corresponding actions. How is this done? By creating a dialogue between the subconscious programming and conscious desires. There are many methods for doing this, but two that I find really powerful are through dream interpretation (understanding the messages coming from your subconscious) and dream therapy (communicating desired changes back to the subconscious).

How can you tell when your subconscious motivations and conscious desires are in alignment? You'll find that there is no longer a resistance to taking the actions that will create that desired outcome. If you're trying to get healthy, then eating right and working out becomes a pleasure instead of a burden. Taking the steps to finish a big project, or bring an invention to life are no longer met with procrastination. Self-sabotage of forward progress is replaced with a well-executed plan of action.

Human Dreaming

The subconscious mind seeks two things: safety and pleasure. Most of your subconscious programming is built between birth and the age of seven, when your brainwaves are mostly in an alpha/theta state. As an adult, theta waves occur when you are dreaming, while in between sleeping and waking states, during meditation or daydreaming, etc. During early childhood, you exist in this imaginative, deep learning state almost all the time. Throughout this developmental period, you are able to learn everything quickly because you are constantly in this malleable state. Your subconscious mind is taking in everything it experiences and using it to lay the foundations of what is perceived as safe and pleasurable.

In adulthood, because your base subconscious programming begins to cement at around age seven, nearly every action you take will be based on what your seven-year-old self thinks is either the safest or most pleasurable course of action. For example, you may stay in that unhealthy relationship until the danger becomes so great that the subconscious decides there must be a safer course of action. For those who subconsciously associate being rewarded or consoled with grandma's delicious cookies, they may grow up to medicate every stressful moment with sugar or carbs, in an attempt to bring back that wonderful pleasure of love through cookies. These associations to what is safe and pleasurable will express themselves in our dreams, and actions.

What exactly are dreams anyway?

There are three main kinds of altered states that can be defined as dreams.

Britt Sheflin

Sleep Dreams

Dreams are real as long as they last. Can we say more of life? – *Napoleon Hill*

The first type of dream we tend to think of is the compilation of various images, emotions, thoughts, and sensations that occur during sleep. Sleep is a period of time when our brains sort all of the information from the day, then send it to communicate with all of the other information stored in our long-term memory. It is this new information, co-mingled with all of the other information deemed pertinent from our memories, that creates the dreams we experience in Rapid Eye Movement sleep.

Sleep dreams have three main categories that we will explore. They are: sorting, predictive, and releasing/reinforcing dreams. Determining dream type is the important first step to dream analysis. Sleep dreams are the main focus of this book; however, you will also learn about lucid dreaming, and other forms of in-between states.

Aspirational Dreams

Man, alone, has the power to transform his thoughts into physical reality; man, alone, can dream and make his dreams come true.
– *Napoleon Hill*

Human Dreaming

Dreams may also occur during waking hours, in the form of an ambition or aspiration to strive for, such as dreaming of becoming a doctor. When this aspiration has been achieved and is being fully appreciated, one might declare they are "living the dream." These types of aspirational dreams often come directly from the conscious mind, and are fulfilled only when our conscious desires are in alignment with our subconscious programming.

The most famous aspirational dream comes from Martin Luther King Jr. His "I have a dream" speech clearly outlines the vision of a future that is within the realm of possibility, and yet is difficult to achieve. Aspirational dreams are often collective, requiring the coordinated effort of an entire community to make the dream a reality.

Fantastical Dreams

> Dreams are excursions into the limbo of things. A semi-deliverance from the human prison.
> *– Henri Amiel*

A third definition of dream is to strongly desire or wish for something that seems unattainable, without necessarily taking real world action to achieve the goal. In other words, this type of dreaming is when we indulge in pure fantasy. Although similar to an ambition, a fantasy typically occurs while in environmental hypnosis, meditation, or while daydreaming. Fantastical dreams are created when conscious desires are supported by subconscious images.

In this book, we will be exploring methods for interpreting sleep dreams. We'll also be exploring how to use the information obtained from sleep dreams to form new aspirational and fantastical dreams.

When I was a kid, I remember my dad saying to me, "anything is possible if you want it badly enough." I loved nothing more than riding my horse, and so taking those words to heart, I would daydream about riding a Pegasus through the sky. I had a deep desire to make this fantasy a reality. The years moved by, and I was no closer to riding a Pegasus through the air, so I became disillusioned with the notion that "anything is possible". Until one day in my 30's, I saw an article about someone who had invented a flying motorcycle with quad copters. It was my mechanical Pegasus! My faith in my dad's statement came flooding back at that moment. Someone else's aspirational dream had made my fantasy a reality.

Sleep dreams can sometimes turn into aspirational dreams. For example, during the point in her life when my midwife, Elizabeth Bachner, was trying to figure out what she wanted to be, she had a dream where she found herself catching babies falling from the sky. After exploring the meaning of the dream, she decided to make helping other women birth safely and comfortably her life's mission.

Sleep dreams are what we interpret from the subconscious, while aspirational and fantastical dreams are the ones we direct consciously. While not all dreams occur during sleeping hours, they all occur in the malleable learning state of alpha/theta brain waves.

Human Dreaming

Why do we need dreams?

Sleep dreams fall into one of three categories: sorting, predictive, or releasing/reinforcing. Sorting is where our subconscious mind decides what is important. Predictive and releasing/reinforcing dreams contain important information presented by the subconscious to the conscious mind. It is these dreams that we generally interpret. When we understand the information being presented to our conscious minds, we have a greater ability to utilize subconscious knowledge in a sentient manner.

One of the main functions of the subconscious mind is to keep us safe by creating homeostasis in our actions. For example, people often take up smoking during their teen years, because it creates a social bond between peers. The subconscious mind now associates cigarettes with positive rewards of camaraderie, relaxation, and acceptance. These associations are further reinforced every time a cigarette is smoked. If the subconscious rapidly changes associations, like the sudden ability to quit smoking, it is for a very good reason. The subconscious decided that the pain of continuing with old habits is more dangerous than making a change. Perhaps the subconscious mind became aware of a detrimental health effect from smoking, or a prospective job or love interest may be put off by smoking.

Whatever the reason, no matter how badly a person wants to quit smoking with their will power, it takes changing the subconscious association to smoking before the behavior modification can take place. The role of the conscious mind is to present logic, reasoning, and willpower to the subconscious mind which in turn checks the programming - is there a positive or negative association to this change? If the two agree, changes are easily made! Dreams play a huge role in releasing what is no longer beneficial to your well-being, and reinforcing what new habits are most likely to provide a sense of security.

During times of processing intense emotions or making a big life change, a lot of especially helpful information will come through our dreams. So, are dreams acting as built-in therapy? Warning signals? Fight/flight/freeze training? Reinforcement of safety behaviors? Creative inspiration? The answer is all of the above.

Why are dreams so integral to being a full-capacity human?

Deep and profound knowledge is housed in the unconscious, and assessing it has great value. Unfortunately, we often sleep through many of the conveyed messages. By writing a dream journal, we are communicating to our unconscious that we are listening and ready to communicate. The more often you write down your dreams, the more frequently you are able to recall them.

When we ignore our dreams, we are potentially ignoring mental, emotional, and physical danger. If ignored long enough, these messages from the subconscious may instead present themselves as anxiety, depression, or various other physical symptoms.

Dreams tell us what our subconscious knows and feels about a particular topic. When we understand their language, they help us release what is no longer helpful, and reinforce new ways of being that benefit us in our current life situation. Conversely, when we don't listen to or understand our dreams,

Human Dreaming

we run the risk of reinforcing what our subconscious is trying to let go.

In western culture, we often cast our sleep dreams aside as a random grouping of nonsensical images. When we continually fail to pay attention to our sleep dreams, we are doing a disservice to our aspirational dreams. Dreams may appear to be entirely symbolic in nature, but by being able to discern the difference between the literal and symbolic aspects of our dreams, we can more easily understand the metaphors contained therein.

An often overlooked, but incredibly important aspect of understanding our dreams is paying attention to our emotions. By using our emotions as the guiding star of dream interpretation (more on this in chapter 6), we are able to navigate the landscape of our emotional lives with grace. Our sleeping hours are often written off as insignificant in comparison to our waking lives. However, dreams are just as real and important in the sense that we viscerally experience them the same way we do waking life, and their emotional impact may last for days, weeks, or longer. By giving the emotions in our dreams the attention that they deserve, we are effectively expanding the hours of the day that hold experiential meaning in our lives beyond just the 16 hours per day that we are awake.

Examining our deep, dark parts, and our most intense and raw emotions is not for the faint of heart, whether we're doing it in our dreams or while awake. When the work is done with conscious intention, there are beautiful nuggets of wisdom and insight to be had from the subconscious sea. Otherwise, we may simply be swimming in our homeostasis, content to keep repeating the same life script while our dreams fall on deaf ears.

Dreams affect our conscious awakenings and vice versa. A dream may give us a bright idea, and when that idea is fulfilled, it may re-enter our dreams as part of our new symbology. When we're moving through life without accessing the 90% of information stored in the subconscious, it's like trying to play a game of poker without seeing your hand. When the conscious and subconscious are in a healthy dialogue, we are able to more easily understand our emotions, solve problems, and see the bigger picture.

How do we begin the dialogue?

Some may find using a visual representation helpful in deconstructing their dreams, so I created the visual aid of the pyramid to help with the concept of building on the interpretation from the foundation up. Journaling your dreams, or even partial dreams in both writing and visual formats stimulates your brain to treat dreams as important, and thus allows dream recall to become automatic.

It takes practice, intention, and repetition, but the reward can be so great. Once we have become adept at dream interpretation and recall, our dreams will respond more readily to requests or suggestions from the conscious mind.

Writing down our dreams upon waking (whether in the middle of the night, or in the morning), is helpful since the moment we change our position, think a new thought, or walk into a new room, we experience what is sometimes referred to as an event threshold, or event boundary. In an instantaneous moment, the change in environment can trigger a whole new series of thoughts and observations of the world around us, causing us to forget what was happening just a moment before. This is frequently associated with forgetting what one was doing when walking into a room, but also applies to dream recall.

Telling the dream aloud to a partner, writing it down, or drawing the dream in a visual representation stimulates an ideomotor phenomenon, an involuntary motion or physical action aided by thoughts or ideas. This may be used as a means of communicating directly with the subconscious mind, which helps us recall our dreams more vividly. By using the ideomotor response, and interpreting the meaning of the dream, we are able to absorb and utilize the information from the dream.

Are All Dreams Important?

Yes, all dreams are feedback of some sort. However, not all dreams need to be fully interpreted. Use the step by step process to determine what type of importance it has. Some dreams need to be interpreted through all seven steps before the significance becomes clear, while other dreams interpretations conclude at step two or three.

There is a spectrum of beliefs about the importance of dreams, ranging from the idea that dreams are completely random and don't really have any value, to every single dream has some sort of intrinsic psychological value or hidden meaning. The reality falls somewhere in between. With Dynamic Dream Interpretation, all dreams are considered to have value, but the type of value may vary widely. Sometimes physical responses enter our dreams, and it is important to interpret them as such so that we're not analyzing a physical stimulus as having a deeper message coming from the subconscious.

Nobody can yet prove where we go when we dream, but what we know is that the brain maintains a high level of activity, even as our bodies rest. Our bodies become still during REM cycles, while our eyes continue to move rapidly. It is this activity that accounts for the physical body, and the electrical impulses of the brain.

Out of body experiences are most often perceived as the soul or essence of who we are becoming untethered from the physical body and being able to move about in space or time. Many people have had out-of-body experiences when sleeping lightly, but also in some cases while in the deeper brainwave states such as in coma. Most report being able to move around near their bodies and view what is happening from a different perspective than from one's own eyes. People experience the moment of coming back "into" the body as a physical sensation. Does the brain need to be active in a specific way for the soul to have the out-of-body experience? Out-of-body experiences, astral projection, and others are common experiences across humanity, but it's difficult to pinpoint exactly where science and metaphysics intersect on this topic.

It is important to pay attention to dreams because they are directly communicating what is important to us. For instance, in a bad relationship, dreams of being shot might mean your safety is at risk (emotional or physical). Dreaming of a loved one giving you a message may be your inner wisdom conveying important information to your conscious mind. Dreams of slow motion running away from an intangible yet scary "bad guy" could mean you need to alter your nutrition (yes, really!).

In order to understand the significance of your dream, a fundamental understanding of the dream framework must first be achieved. Learning about your dreams can take the scariness out of nightmares, and sleep paralysis. It can remove the guilt from doing things in your dreams that you would never do in real life. It gives us insight into what may be preventing us from taking desirable actions, and also what positive traits we want to reinforce in ourselves.

Britt Sheflin

Key Takeaways

By understanding the language of our subconscious minds via dreams, and creating a dialogue between conscious and subconscious through journaling, we are able to:

- Perceive our sleeping life with equal importance as our waking life
- Live more intentionally. Instead of running on old programming, we can direct our waking lives more frequently with our conscious minds
- Tap into the powerful resource that is our unconscious, in order to direct changes to our subconscious life script
- Identify the different types of dreams
    - Sleep
    - Aspirational
    - Fantastical
- Know when we're making choices subconsciously, or consciously
- Find ways to utilize our dreams for creativity and problem solving

When implementing Dynamic Dream Interpretation into your daily life, you may begin to see the cycle of human dreaming, human doing, human being in action.

Chapter 2 – Life Script

I can never decide whether my dreams are the result of my thoughts, or my thoughts the result of my dreams. – D. H. Lawrence

What is your life script, and what does it have to do with understanding the meaning of your dreams? Your life script determines your dreams, actions, and personality. Luckily, you can decide whether the script should remain as is, or make some adjustments.

Your life script is the story of you - your sense of self in the form of thoughts, feelings, and behaviors. It runs in the background at all times, whether sleeping or awake. It determines nearly every action you take. Every triumph, every failure, every pull-yourself-up-by-the-bootstraps moment, and every self-sabotage is due, in some part, to your life script. It is what you tell yourself about who you are.

Your life script comes out while awake, in the form of looping thoughts (repetitive thoughts that are often unwanted or unkind to yourself) and repetitive actions or habits. If your looping thoughts are consistently negative or self-deprecating, that will affect the actions you take, both in dreams, and in waking life. If the tendency is to use your imagination to daydream scenarios full of worrisome occurrences, the subconscious is in a reactive fight/flight mode, and may need assistance in redirecting these patterns. Similarly, your repetitive actions are also coming from your life script. Your subconscious mind dictates how you feel you deserve to take care of yourself in all aspects of your life from grooming to sleep habits, to forming healthy boundaries.

We are responsible for enacting and editing our life script. Interestingly, the original script is largely written by our culture and those we are exposed to at a young age. Parents, teachers, siblings, and friends, all contribute heavily to our life script. Other factors may contribute to a lesser degree. Epigenetics are the mechanism by which things like fear of snakes, ptsd, and certain food preferences can be passed down biologically. Environmental factors can stem from growing up isolated from or exposed to the greater world. Our own inherent uniqueness of personality is also a factor.

Although life scripts may be largely written by others, they can only be edited or overwritten by you. One technique for altering your life script is creating a dialogue with the subconscious via your dreams. Teaching your conscious mind to be the director of your subconscious programming changes your life outcomes.

Life scripts are stored in the subconscious, and appear in the form of dreams when sleeping. While awake they take the form of daydreams, automated actions, and looping thoughts. Life scripts can be brought into the conscious mind by becoming aware of the repeating thoughts flowing through our mind and deciding whether or not to edit them.

In the physical sense, the whole brain is both conscious and subconscious. However, the subconscious is primarily housed in the limbic system, which hosts the emotional centers, endocrine systems, memory, learning, and nervous system responses. The conscious mind operates mostly out of the prefrontal cortex where the more executive functions of logic, reasoning, and willpower occur. Looping thoughts in the brain may become stronger over time. There is a saying, "the neurons that fire together, wire together", meaning our thoughts build physical structures in our brains. In order to edit our life script, we need our prefrontal cortex to become aware of what the rest of the brain is doing, and then consistently over time encourage these new thoughts to fire and wire together. By creating a more pleasant and fruitful inner dialogue, we guide our subconscious programming to work in favor of taking the necessary actions to fulfill our conscious desires.

Famed psychologist, Erik Erikson, developed the psychosocial stages of development that describes how mental and emotional milestones occur at certain ages. Around the age of seven is when most people transition from the Initiative vs Guilt stage, when ambition and responsibility are developed. They then enter the Industry vs Inferiority stage, when children begin to compare themselves to their peers. This transition point is also where a lot of our subconscious perceptions of the world become ingrained. The culture and family we are born to greatly determine the type of foundation we have in these stages of development. If as a child, you developed a fundamental distrust of adults, but a strong sense of autonomy, your life script, and consequently your dreams, will be fundamentally different than if you had a solid foundation in both trust and autonomy.

To alter a life script, we must first identify those things which we say to ourselves about ourselves. Until you learn how to interpret the information that comes from the subconscious, it can sometimes be a challenge. The easiest ways to identify elements of your life script on your own are to a) pinpoint and write down what your negative looping thoughts and worries are, and to b) write down and interpret your dreams.

Once the various parts of your life script have been identified, begin to edit the script by outlining your desired outcome, and all of the steps it will take to get there. Do not hold back! Rewrite your script, and memorize and embody the new changes as if you were a method actor about to play the biggest role of your life. With consistency, these changes will be noticed in the subconscious mind, allowing change to occur.

Role-model tip

If you would like to give children the gift of a healthy life script, watch not only how you talk to them, but how you talk about yourself and others. The words you use about yourself and others, become their thoughts about how they perceive themselves.

In my hypnotherapy practice, I help people edit their life scripts by imagining a better future together. If a pregnant person comes to me with a life script that childbirth is supposed to be a horrible and traumatic experience, I help them rewrite their subconscious programming to perceive childbirth in a new way. If my client believes that they are unworthy of their success, together we collaborate on a plan to replace imposter syndrome with confidence, thus modifying their life script. One of the most common scripts is the simultaneous fear of failure and success, which creates an overwhelming feeling of mediocrity. This challenge can be overcome by giving the subconscious pleasurable responses to incremental steps towards the desired outcome. There is one solution all of my clients have in common: the conscious mind needs to see a clear picture of the desired outcome first. We identify the current script, detail the best possible result, then work backwards towards creating actions from there.

The positive parts of my life script were given to me from my parents and grandparents who all told me I was intelligent, a talented creative, and could do anything I wanted. Whether I actually was talented at five is highly questionable, but they reinforced that thought in my mind repeatedly. They told me I had an eye for art, that they enjoyed my writing, and that it was okay to be unconventional. My family members not only said positive and encouraging things to me, but they also spoke highly of others. They gave me this gift in the form of repetition, which in turn, became my own inner thoughts. Once I accepted that as my script, it became further reinforced.

The positive parts of my life script told me I could thrive in an unconventional life in off-grid treehouses, learn permaculture, and how to forage for natural foods and craft supplies. My life script instilled in me the belief that I could reinvent myself over and over again pursuing my aspirations of being a clothing designer, jewelry maker, fire dance performer, private chef, filmmaker, and finally, a hypnotherapist and author. My negative scripts were also handed to me in the form of the self-talk I heard from my relatives, teachers, and mentors, primarily about how their bodies were flawed, and how money is hard to come by. Although I heard a lot of praise for myself and others, I also internalized a lot of the self-criticism I heard from those same relatives. With our own daughter, my partner and

I are cautious of how we talk about ourselves and others in front of her.

Interestingly, our daughter didn't know what nightmares were and until the age of five when her best friend mentioned a bad dream she'd had. My daughter was not excited to learn about the existence of scary dreams, but despite all that, she continues to talk about her dreams, laugh in her sleep, and has had only one nightmare that I know of. Since she is under seven, this type of comedic dreaming is mostly built into her personality. She also processes a lot of her internal conflicts through play and daydreaming. Perhaps most importantly, we feed her very little sugar, and offer her the opportunity to eat one last healthy thing right before brushing teeth at night. Nutrition plays a huge role in the formation of certain types of nightmares, but more on that later.

The life script you are born with is not the final version. It is a rough draft of a story that can sit ignored on a dusty shelf, or you can learn how to edit it to suit your tastes. Everyone is dealt a different script at birth. And you, as the director, can only put on that one play, or make that one movie for your entire life. You may have been handed a real stinker of a script, but the more you learn how to refine it, the more you have the ability to take a terrible story and make it meaningful. Eventually, you will have a production that is adept at making the necessary changes to the story safely, with flexibility, and precision. Learning your life script is a prerequisite to more fully understanding your dreams. Once you are familiar with your script, Dynamic Dream Interpretation can be used to create a constructive dialogue between your subconscious actor, and your conscious director. Your dreams will thank you for getting to know them better.

Human Dreaming

Key Takeaways

- Your life script is the story of you, and determines the actions you will take to fulfill that story
- Your life script is performed in both dream and awake states
- To learn your script, first identify and write down your subconscious patterns:
    - Daydreams: Are your daydreams pleasant escapes, or are you using your creative mind to worry?
    - Automatic actions: What do you frequently find yourself doing that is not a conscious decision? It could be suddenly noticing that you're eating something unhealthy, that you crack your knuckles, or get distracted when it's time to get stuff done.
    - Looping thoughts: We've all had them. "I'm not good enough. Somebody else is better. I'm too fat/skinny. Who do I think I am to put myself out there like that? I'll never be as good as _____." The list goes on... Can you identify your looping thoughts?
- By learning your life script, you begin to understand the language your subconscious mind speaks, and you start to have more control over it
- Sleeping dreams and waking dreams are different, yet connected in important ways

Once you know what your life script is, and you learn how to make editing notes, you can finally become the conscious director of your own play, and your subconscious mind becomes the supporting actors (instead of the other way around). Having gained an understanding of your life script, you now explore the different aspects of dreams, which ones are helpful for interpretation, and which ones have no psychological basis for interpretation.

Chapter 3 – Your Own Expert

One can write, think, and pray exclusively of others; dreams are all egocentric. – *Evelyn Waugh*

Imagine having a powerful dream that you know holds some deep meaning for you. But you just can't seem to understand the language in which it's being told. You know that your mother flying away in a hot air balloon represents something, but what exactly? So you purchase a dream interpretation book. The book says the hot air balloon represents unattainable goals. But that doesn't seem quite right because several years back you experienced an overwhelming sense of freedom riding in a hot air balloon for the first time. As a result, your association to hot air balloons is a positive one. What could this dream mean?

You are your own expert. Only you can know what your own symbology truly means. Once interpreted, other people may help you gain additional insight into those dreams, but you are the only one who can answer the questions that will lead to an accurate interpretation of your own dream. Get curious about what benefits a collaborative mind can provide you!

I often help my clients discover the meaning of their dreams, but only by way of helping them decipher their own symbology. I still guide them through the same process they could do for themselves, I simply provide them with the tools, and give additional insight when needed.

People tend to want instant answers for their dreams. Unfortunately, there are no quick answers for an accurate dream interpretation. However, once you begin to learn the inner workings of your own subconscious, it's like learning a musical instrument or a new language. At first the learning curve is steep, but once you get the hang of it, it becomes second nature, and you don't have to work so hard at analyzing each aspect. Eventually, when you wake up you will have a pretty clear (and nearly instant) understanding of your own subconscious messages.

> I've always been fascinated by memory and dreams because they are completely our own. No one else has the same memories. No one else has the same dreams. – *Lois Lowry*

Sometimes people believe they want to know the answer to what a dream is telling them. But as with any growth or change, there can be resistance to acknowledging the hard truths represented in your dreams. It's often easier for people to go with the one-size-fits all interpretation from a dream book, or well-intended friend who offers up a possible meaning. And sometimes those dream books or friends' interpretations can hold a grain of truth. But if your goal is to get to know your own subconscious language, to push the boundaries of your personal growth and change, then learning how to interpret your own dreams is an incredibly powerful tool to add to your skillset.

Subconscious Symbology applies to all of the aspects of dream interpretation. However, the symbols themselves only account for a portion of the deeper meaning of the dream. We must also be aware of the emotions, literal aspects, timing clues, and physiological stimulus in order to fully understand our dreams.

Sometimes, one aspect of a dream may hold more power than the other parts. But to discover the relative magnitude of a dream component, all of the questions need to be asked in order. For example, in one dream the emotions may play the key role in letting you know what your dream means. In another dream, it may be the dream type that holds the key to understanding. In yet another, it may be knowing what the literal aspects are that brings the symbology into focus. Sometimes it is a more even balance of all of these parts, and each answer holds equal importance.

When I help my clients with an analysis, I allow them to be their own expert: "Mary" had a dream about breaking down on the side of the road. Through the discovery process, we learned it was a predictive dream. When we examined what else was going on in her life, I learned that she was about to embark on a cross-country journey that would include towing a trailer. Only Mary knew her inner thoughts, but the clues she provided led to discussions on why she might be having this particular predictive dream, and what it might be trying to prepare her for.

As it turned it out, there was something wrong with the towing system that her subconscious mind had picked up on, but had not yet made it to her conscious awareness. By thoroughly examining the dream she was able to ensure that all of her towing and safety systems were properly functioning, thus avoiding what may have been a "dream come true".

Key Takeaways

- Once interpreted, other people may help you gain insights to your dreams, but only you will truly know what your subconscious symbology is referring to. You are your own expert.
- Answering all of the Dynamic Dream Interpretation questions in order builds a solid foundation from which to understand your dream.
- Be curious about what your subconscious is trying to communicate.
- Some aspects of any given dream may hold more meaning than others. Follow the clues to discover which aspects may hold more weight.

Next time you have a powerful dream where the meaning is not immediately clear, use this book to help you tease out accurate information. The first step of Dynamic Dream Interpretation is learning what type of dream you're having.

Human Dreaming

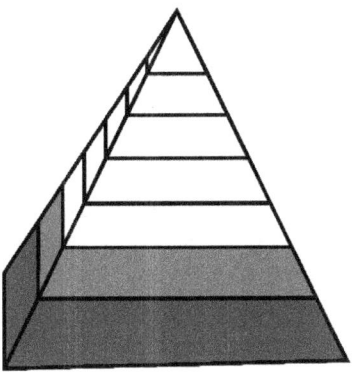

Chapter 4 – Steps 1 & 2: Dream Types and Subtypes

We are such stuff as dreams are made on, and our
little life is rounded with a dream.
– *William Shakespeare*

Have you ever had a dream where you're running in place, terrified, but nothing changes no matter how hard you run? Perhaps a dream that is so insistent, it keeps repeating itself? Have you ever been watching a movie, and had the contents of the film enter your dream?

Understanding the type of dream you're having is the most important factor in understanding the content of your dream. It is the first step you will take in interpreting the dream, and is the foundation of understanding your Subconscious Symbology. There are many clues to help guide you in determining which type of dream you're having. These are not stringent rules, but rather guidelines that will help you to determine the most fundamental question of dream interpretation: What type of dream did I have, and what does that information tell me in relation to all of the other aspects of my dream?

Research has shown that humans tend to dream in approximately 90-minute REM cycles. The stages of dreaming, especially the predictive and releasing/reinforcing dreams, tend to last closer to two REM cycles, and may account for why we sometimes recall multiple dreams about different things. Depending how quickly you go into each cycle, and how long you sleep for, will affect what stages of dreams you experience, and at what times. Since length and quality of sleep may vary, there are no set rules regarding when in the night each dream type occurs. The timing of the dream provides clues based on what you know about your own sleep patterns. If you regularly have a perfect eight hours of sleep and you go to bed at 10 pm every night, your dream stages would look like this:

- 10 pm - 12 am Sorting
- 12 am - 3 am Predictive
- 3 am - 6 am Releasing/Reinforcing

It may take a bit more investigating of the dream subtypes before you're able to discern whether or not you had a predictive or releasing/reinforcing dream. For instance, if you went to bed at 10 pm and woke up at 3:15 am, you may still have been in the predictive stage, or you may have already transitioned into the releasing/reinforcing stage. Similarly, if you are someone who only needs 6 hours of sleep per night, you will need to adjust your timing. Writing consistently in your dream journal, and familiarizing yourself with your sleep patterns, will give you greater insight into which stage of

Human Dreaming

dreaming you're in. By following the clues provided to identify your dream type and subtype, you are establishing the foundational step in building your dream interpretation.

Dream Types

Sorting: Sorting dreams occur in the first stages of dreaming. They are very rarely recalled, and if they are, may not have a very clear storyline. The purpose of a sorting dream is to take all of the information from the day, compare it to previous experiences from your life, and then categorize it into useful information to be stored, or obsolete information to be deleted. A strong clue that you had a sorting dream is that it happened within the first couple of hours of falling asleep. Due to their lack of clarity, sorting dreams are not typically used for analysis. If you have a dream with a very clear storyline during the first hour or two of sleep, it may be due to poor sleep patterns. If consistent deep sleep is not happening, the brain will drop into deep REM much faster than usual, thus accelerating past the sorting stage and into predictive and/or releasing/reinforcing.

Predictive: Predictive dreams tend to occur in the middle of the sleep cycle, or about 3-5 hours into a full night of sleeping. They are not easy to recall unless immediately documented. This stage of dreaming serves to create practice events for your subconscious to run through in order to be better prepared for what it calculates are likely scenarios you'll face. Much like how athletes repeatedly practice their high-level skills mentally before executing them physically, the subconscious likes to be prepared. This is why certain types of nightmares occur during this stage. If you're prepared for the worst in dreams, when it happens in real life you will have had some practice beforehand at dealing with the situation.

Predictive dreams can have potent warnings for us, yet they are not as easily remembered as releasing and reinforcing dreams. These forecasting dreams serve two main functions:

1. they give us the opportunity to react to plausible scenarios created by the subconscious mind; adding up all of the variables of possibility, in a safe and repetitive environment, and;
2. they may warn us about actual impending events that involve physical or emotional pain.

It is common for the subconscious mind to be aware of dangers such as domestic abuse, or overlooked safety precautions, far before we become consciously aware of them. If you wake in the middle of the night, and have an intense dream with a clear beginning, middle, and end, that is a signal that the predictive dream is important to write down and interpret right away.

Releasing and reinforcing dreams: Releasing and reinforcing dreams happen in the 2-3 hours before waking. They are a direct message from the subconscious about what it deems important to release or reinforce. Because these dreams tend to occur 2-3 hours before waking, these are the easiest type of dreams to remember. As the name implies, releasing and reinforcing dreams occur in order to either:

Human Dreaming

a. release thoughts, feelings, and behaviors that the subconscious is ready to let go of, or;
b. reinforce new behaviors that the subconscious deems important.

Most of the time only releasing dreams are interpreted, since they are made up of emotions that need to be processed. When releasing dreams are not interpreted, there is a risk of reinforcing the negative associations instead of venting them out.

People rarely try to interpret the reinforcing aspect of this dream type, as they typically are of the feel-good variety, and it may not seem as pressing as the more emotionally charged releasing dream. These enjoyable dreams are signaling what you are subconsciously reinforcing as positive associations to new experiences or behaviors. You might have these kinds of dreams when a newer activity becomes an enjoyable habit, when you have spent precious time with a loved one, or are about to go on a much-needed vacation.

Dream Subtypes

Dream subtypes are the second layer, added to the foundation of the main dream type. Depending on which main category your dream falls under, your dream subtype may provide a different context.

If, during the course of an interpretation, the dream subtype isn't immediately obvious, that's a clue that it is most likely the "present" subtype. The dream subtype "present" just means that the subconscious is processing emotions and experiences from the present, or very recent past. Most dreams fall under this category. Clues that point to a dream being about something other than the present, are when you dream as a younger (past) or older (future) version of yourself. If many elements from a specific time period in your life appear, they are hinting at specific events during that time period, so you may add "past, present, or future" to your subtype(s).

These are some of the most common dream subtypes:

Recurring dreams are an important subtype to pay attention to. If a dream is coming back to you repeatedly, it's the subconscious mind alerting you to pay attention. Recurring dreams can go on for weeks, months, or years, or until the underlying cause is addressed. It is recommended to always thoroughly interpret recurring dreams.

Nightmares are a subtype of dream that center around scary, sad, or overwhelming emotions. Typically, they fall under the predictive or releasing categories. When a nightmare is predictive, it's usually your brain practicing for what it predicts might be hard times, or it could be a warning that you need to take conscious action to change your situation. When clues point to the nightmare being a releasing dream, then it is important to thoroughly interpret it so that you don't risk reinforcing what the subconscious is trying to let go of. Once you understand what your subconscious is trying to release, then the emotions of the nightmare lose steam, and you are able to vent out something you may have been holding onto for a long time.

Human Dreaming

Lucid dreams can be fun and exciting! Tending towards intensely visual, they are usually fully recalled, and often occur right before waking. Since they are controlled in large part by the conscious mind, with minimal subconscious input, it is not recommended to interpret them. Additionally, unless you have chronic sleep paralysis (an often-unpleasant version of lucid dreaming), it doesn't make sense to start training to lucid dream until you are adept at interpreting dreams and messages that come directly from your deep-sleep dreams. Once you are able to clearly understand the messages coming from subconscious dreams, then it is a good time to play with lucid dreaming. Other types of experiences and terms that fall under the lucid dreaming category include:

- Remote viewing (seeing something or someone physically far away from you but in the current time)
- Astral projection (seeing different times, dimensions, etc.)
- Hypnagogic reverie (the pleasant state of relaxation that often occurs just before falling asleep where trance, meditative imagery, or fantasy may occur)
- Daydreaming (waking "dream" where mental visuals may be augmented over reality, highly detailed daytime fantasy)

All of these experiences fall under the same category of lucid dreaming because they are occurring in the space between waking and sleeping, when the brain is anywhere between a light alpha to deep theta state. Daydreaming occurs closer to a fully awake state, lucid dreaming occurs closer to sleeping, and the others help form the assemblage point between and around the other alpha/theta state experiences.

Sleep Paralysis often occurs during the twilight times of falling asleep and waking. It is a type of lucid dream, where the mind is semi-awake, but the body is still "paralyzed" as if in a deep sleep. The brain uses what is theorized to be a combination of gamma-aminobutyric acid and glycine to turn off the cells in the brain that permit movement of muscles. In essence, being immobilized during sleep is an overall evolutionary benefit that helps keep us (and our bed partners) safe, by making all of our muscles still; except those used for critical processes such as breathing, and rapid eye movement. However, it can go awry when the body and brain sleep/wake cycles are not in sync, thus causing the experience of sleep paralysis. Some people experience sleep paralysis as scary because:

a) they haven't learned how to control it yet (feeling as if you cannot move, can be panic inducing), and
b) there is a worldwide hallucinatory phenomena surrounding sleep paralysis experiences, where people see and sometimes feel an entity sitting on their chest, or even choking them.

Through lucid dreaming training (becoming aware of when you're dreaming, and taking control of the dream), sleep paralysis may be mitigated.

Sexual dreams can occur for a variety of reasons. If they are fun and pleasant, it may be a reinforcing or predictive dream surrounding your sexuality. They can also occur during times of heightened hormones (such as puberty), in which case they might be a purely physiological dream. If the sexual dream is frustrating, or unpleasant, you may want to explore whether it's a releasing dream, and examine where else in your life you're experiencing frustration of any nature. The meaning of the dream doesn't have to have to stem from the sexual arena, it could be work-related, family-related, creative frustration, etc.

Creative dreams often fall under the category of releasing/reinforcing dreams, and may provide insight into your coping mechanisms, and/or things you are ready to let go of. It may also be a dream that you can utilize in your work - such as a comedic dream helping to form a new joke or standup routine for a comedian, or solving a design problem for an architect, or coming up with a lighting setup for that perfect photograph.

Anxiety dreams are often work related, though they can stem from anywhere in your life you may be experiencing discomfort, or are sensing loss of control. Anyone who has ever waited tables has likely had a generalized anxiety dream that makes them feel like they were at work all night. Impostor syndrome, fears of failure, and/or success, are frequently experienced as anxiety dreams. Other common manifestations of anxiety are teeth crumbling and falling dreams.

Spiritual and ancestor dreams can come in many forms. They are often tied to a person's spiritual or religious beliefs. A visitation from a deceased loved one, a future child, or former self, are frequent among some dreamers. Occasionally, there have been reports of past-life type dreams where a person experiences a completely different religion, culture, and family life, only to open their eyes and transform back into their waking belief systems.

Some people believe that they have absorbed or accumulated the wisdom from that ancestor into their own subconscious intelligence, and some believe that their ancestor is actually visiting them in non-corporeal form, dealing out wisdom and love from another dimension.

Collective dreams occur when large groups of people are dreaming about the same symbology. Because we experience life collectively, as well as individually, we also can dream common themes. Oftentimes, collective dreaming will occur during a period of great change. In 2016, for example, clinical psychologist Martha Crawford documented over 3000 dreams about the 45th U.S. president, who had quickly and definitively become a subconscious symbol in the dreams of many Americans. As I write this during the COVID-19 pandemic, people are frequently dreaming about not having their face masks, being coughed on, or otherwise exposed to the virus.

Joyful dreams tend to go under the reinforcing category, however they may also be predictive. Many people choose not to interpret joyful dreams, but they can be just as fun to explore as the more unpleasant or bizarre dreams.

Physiological dreams are ones where outside influences such as noises, blood sugar drops, or hormone fluctuations take control of the dream. Physiological dreams are not necessary to interpret, since they do not have a psychological basis (see more in Chapter 5).

Psychological dreams are communications coming directly from the subconscious, and usually contain emotions that relate to experiences you're having in waking life. These are the important dreams to interpret. Psychological dreams are widely varied in content (see more in Chapter 5).

Nap dreams, hypnagogic reverie, daydreams, and lucid dreams may be normal nap time experiences, however, if you're dropping into an REM dreaming cycle during a nap, it may be a sign that you're not getting enough deep sleep at night, or there is another underlying sleep issue. If you are having regular sleep dreams during nap times, it may be an indication of an imbalance that needs attention. Please consider bringing it up with your physician, or joining a sleep study.

Past. Dreams about the past, or of yourself as a younger person are giving you hints that you are processing something from that period of time in your life. Past dreams tend to fall into the releasing/reinforcing stage of dreaming.

Future. Dreams where you are an older version of yourself can be predictive, but are also just as likely to be releasing/reinforcing in nature. Regardless of which main dream type it is, this subtype is looking to the future.

Present. The most powerful clue that you're having a dream about the present is that you are experiencing it as yourself, at your own age. Most dreams fall under the category of dealing with the present or a very recent past. It is comparatively rare to have distant past or future dreams. If you're unsure of what age you are, it is most likely current, as the subconscious tends to make a different age a key factor of a past or future dream. If it's not obvious that you're someone or something else in the dream, then you can presume you were yourself.

Parallel. Set in the here and now, parallel dreams feature you as someone or something else (ex: a wolf, bird, or even an inanimate object). Typically, these are about the here and now, and may point to concerns about an aspect of yourself, or about someone else very close to you. The what and why will become apparent further on into building the layers of your dream interpretation, after you have determined the physiological, psychological, literal, and symbolic aspects, as well as mapped the emotional arc of the dream.

In order to fully understand what messages the subconscious mind is sending, a person needs to know the difference between predictive and releasing/reinforcing dreams. For example, if someone dreams that their partner is going to leave them, depending on when the dream occurred, it could mean different things. If it occurred during the predictive stage, it likely means that there are signals the dreamer has been picking up unconsciously from their partner, and the subconscious knows the partner is unhappy about some aspect of the relationship.

Alternatively, it could mean more literally that the partner is planning to leave (or your subconscious thinks you should leave for your own safety), and the dreamer's conscious mind simply hasn't picked up on the signals. If the dream occurred during the releasing/reinforcing phase, it is likely to mean something entirely different, and may not be related to the romantic relationship at all, but rather the destruction of the relationship may be serving as a symbol for something else that's going on in waking life, and may not even be paired with the dreamer's love life.

Human Dreaming

Recently - and much like the time I had the intuition about the car accident - I had a predictive, or intuitive, dream about an incident where our five-year-old was not where she was supposed to be, and was in physical danger. I had forgotten about the dream until it was almost time to go pick her up from a relative's house. Recalling the intensity of the dream, I hurried over there and arrived a couple minutes early. As soon as I stepped onto the porch, the overwhelming fear and dread of the dream came flooding back. When the door went unanswered, I knew I'd had a predictive dream and my intuition was trying to warn me about a possible danger.

When my relatives had arrived back at the house, I immediately saw what my subconscious had picked up on, and why I'd had the dream: she was sitting in the front seat of their vehicle without a proper restraint system. I was not consciously aware that they were taking her out on errands without informing us, but somehow my subconscious mind had picked up on enough clues to tell my conscious mind that standard safety protocols were not being followed. Understanding that information presented to me in my dreams directed me to prevent further unsafe incidents from occurring.

Key Takeaways

- Knowing your dream type is the foundation of building your dream pyramid
- The three main dream types are: sorting, predictive, releasing/reinforcing. Each occurs at three different intervals during the night
- Use timing hints and other clues to help determine which type and subtype of dream(s) you experienced
- If not interpreted, psychological dreams run the risk of reinforcing a negative experience
- Releasing/reinforcing dreams are the most commonly remembered dreams. They give us the most feedback on what we're ready to release, and what is healthy to keep in our lives

Now that you know how to pinpoint your dream type and subtype, you're ready to build on the next layer, determining the physiological and psychological aspects of your dreams.

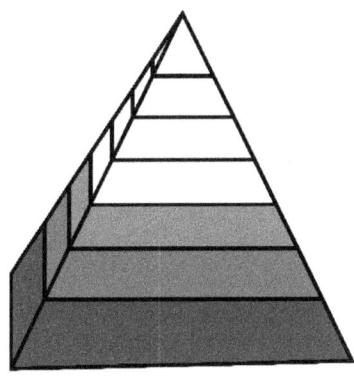

Chapter 5 – Step 3: Physiological and Psychological Aspects

Dreams are the guiding words of the soul. Why should I henceforth not love my dreams and not make their riddling images into objects of my daily consideration? – Carl Jung

When information and stimulus from the outside world is intermingling with our internal subconscious dialogue, the messages can get distorted, or interrupted. If you're having a physiological dream, it's not important to analyze the psychological meaning behind it, because it's composed of outside stimulus and is being presented to a partially conscious mind.

There are two main causes of physiological dreams. The first is a light state of sleep where external stimulus from sounds, smells, or sensations can enter the dreamscape and interrupt the messages from the subconscious. At this point we're likely in a semi-lucid state, and it's difficult to determine whether or not the information is coming from the subconscious, or from the conscious awareness of our surroundings. This, along with the fact that we shouldn't be dropping into REM, is another reason why napping dreams are rarely interpreted.

The second cause of a physiological dream is a blood sugar crash while in a deep state of sleep. Low blood sugar dreams tend to occur in the middle of the night, and frequently result in nightmares. Often these dreams will have no clear beginning, middle or end. Other signs that strongly point to physiological interference are: sweating, shaking, uncontrollable emotions, sobbing, and panic attacks. These are important clues, especially if you had the dream during the predictive stage.

That being said, while physiological dreams are not worth interpreting in the psychological sense, they may provide other valuable feedback. Sometimes the best ideas and inventions come from the semi-lucid state of physiological dreams! The body is relaxed enough to be asleep, but the mind is still at least partially aware, and creativity is heightened.

During the course of writing this book, my mom was having intense nightmares. The dreams got so bad that she became afraid to go to sleep. My stepdad had recently passed, so initially we both thought her dreams and sleeplessness were due to processing grief. Upon closer examination, we discovered that in these dreams she would be endlessly running away from something/someone, fearing for her life. There was no clear middle, beginning, or end to these dreams. She would then wake up in the middle of the night sweaty, shaking, and terrified.

Human Dreaming

After discussing her dreams and discovering these clues, we determined that these dreams were not worth interpreting, because they had a physiological basis. Knowing the dreams were not worth interpreting was one thing, but how else was this information useful? This is where it got interesting. Upon asking my mom about her eating habits in the hours before bed I learned that she was, understandably, soothing her grief with desserts before bed. This was causing her to have a blood sugar crash in the middle of the night.

The symptoms of low blood sugar include shakiness, anxiety, excess sweating, discomfort (and in some cases violence), plus a whole host of other unpleasant fight/flight related effects. During the day, we may have the awareness that we're "hangry", and quickly eat something, nearly immediately relieving the symptoms of low blood sugar. During sleep, however, our bodies notify us of the problem through our dreams by sending increasingly urgent messages in the form of physical and emotional pain. When the blood sugar drops to a critical point, we are no longer in a resting state where our minds can sort out our thoughts and create meaningful dreams. Instead we enter full-blown fight/flight mode, often resulting in nightmares.

So, instead of an emotionally comforting nighttime sweet treat, my mom replaced her desserts with a more nourishing snack. As a result, the nightmares immediately vanished and she was able to return to normal sleep cycles. Thereafter, she kept eggs, nuts, and other foods with high protein and healthy fats on hand. It is high protein and healthy fat foods such as these that promoted blood sugar stabilization, and prevented the nightmares from returning.

Once you are able to identify this type of physiologically-based dream, it lets the emotional steam out of the nightmare and you'll be able to release it much faster, since you know that it isn't coming from your subconscious. You'll also have the benefit of learning how to prevent them. If you already eat a very low-sugar/high-protein/healthy-fats diet and continue having these types of nightmares, it's important to speak to your doctor, as there may be an underlying condition.

If you have recurring physiological nightmares and don't address your nutrition, you may not only continue having blood sugar crashes in your sleep, but also run the risk of developing trauma, chronic insomnia, or extreme phobias.

While the conscious mind rests, the subconscious is on duty 24/7. In order to receive psychological messages from the subconscious, we need to either be:

a) in a deep dream state, or
b) in an intentional dialogue with the subconscious.

Outside of dreaming, you can achieve a constructive dialogue with the subconscious in several ways, including being in session with your hypnotherapist, doing therapeutic guided imagery with your psychologist, or keeping a detailed journal of your repetitive thoughts, and editing them accordingly. Hypnotherapy and guided imagery are perhaps the easiest ways of creating a dialogue with the subconscious outside of dreaming hours, but tracking and editing your inner dialogue is also effective when practiced regularly.

Human Dreaming

Not all dreams are created equal in terms of psychological value. Imagine a dream where you're being slimed by a monster, only to wake up to excited kisses from a pet? Have you ever had a dream where you're running in place, feeling fear, but nothing else happens? There's no real story in your dream, just a bad feeling, and a repetitive, futile action? These are both examples of physiological dreams, and because they come from external stimuli, they are not generally useful to dream interpretation. The third step in building your dream interpretation is determining whether you are experiencing subconscious dialogue or external stimulus. If it is subconscious dialogue (holding psychological value), you may continue with the interpretation.

Typically dreams that are worth interpreting to completion come from deep to medium REM cycles. The lighter the sleep, the more likely it is that you're in a semi-lucid state, when external input is more likely to play into the dreamscape than subconscious symbology.

In addition to blood sugar levels having a significant impact on dream quality, substances also play a role in influencing our experiences. Here are a few of the more well-known dream-altering substances:

Cheese. Containing tryptophan, and various b vitamins that are also associated with sleep, cheese eaten before bed does not appear to affect the type of dream, but has been known to make them more vivid.

Cannabis. It is often associated with suppression of dream recall. Not an ideal substance to consume if you're trying to remember more dreams, but may be a good tool if you're trying to sleep more soundly, or avoid dream recall.

Opioids. These substances may especially interfere with the later stages of dreaming. They have been known to contribute to experiencing especially vivid nightmares.

Hormones. Since hormones naturally occur in the body, there's not too much that can be done to avoid them from affecting your dreams, but it is good to be aware of what role they play. During times of extreme hormonal changes such as puberty, pregnancy, and menopause, dreams can become more intense than usual. This is a physiological aspect of dreaming. It doesn't mean that your dream doesn't have psychological importance, but it does mean that the intensity of your dreams may be heightened. When interpreting a dream with hormonal aspects, you can mark the dream as both psychological and physiological. Unlike a dream caused by blood sugar drops, hormonal dreams that have a clear beginning, middle, and end, and so still hold valuable information for interpretation.

Other substances that may alter your dreamscape are: pharmaceutical drugs such as Ambien, antidepressants, some blood pressure medications, and beta-blockers, as well as recreational drugs such as cocaine, MDMA, and caffeine, among others. That is not to say that you won't still have good psychological information while on dream-altering substances, but it is good to be aware of how they may be affecting the intensity and recall of your dreams.

Human Dreaming

Key Takeaways

- If you've gone through the first 3 steps:
  a) dream type
  b) dream subtype
  c) physiological/psychological aspects
  and had a Psychological dream, continue to steps 4 - 7.
- If you've had a Physiological dream, no need to continue the dream interpretation - instead look to external factors such as household noise, pets, or stabilizing blood sugar.
- Nutrition plays a large role in sleeping well and staving off certain types of nightmares.
- The substances and medications we consume affect our dreams. Understand how your body reacts to these.... This will help contribute valuable clues as you build your dream interpretation.

The next time you have a dream about getting slimed, or a particularly horrible nightmare, verify what physiological factors may be at play before continuing. If you have determined your dream to be psychological in nature, you may move on to step 4 - identifying the emotions in your dream.

Britt Sheflin

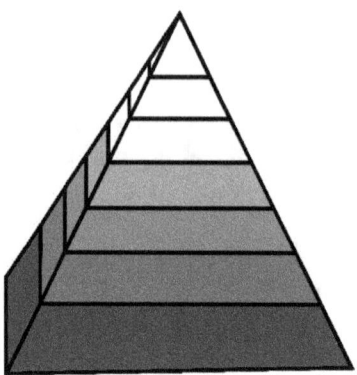

Chapter 6 – Step 4: Emotions Are Your Guide

I was not looking for my dreams to interpret my life,
but rather for my life to interpret my dreams.
– *Susan Sontag*

When it comes to dream interpretation, emotions are your guide, your compass, your lodestar. If you were to imagine building your dream interpretation in the form of a seven layer pyramid, the foundation is the dream type. The second step is the dream subtype. The third step is determining the physiological and psychological aspects. If a dream has been determined to have psychological value, you can continue building the fourth layer, by examining the emotional content of the dream. It's this central fourth layer where the most important messages are stored, and the most important factor in understanding a psychological dream.

Human Dreaming

Emotions are an essential component of understanding your dreams. Experiencing powerful emotions in a dream is how your subconscious communicates directly about what is being processed. While most of the visual aspects of our dreams are highly symbolic, our emotions point more literally to what the dream is about.

We tend to remember with great accuracy how we felt even in our distant memories, but our recall of what was said or done is less clear. Emotions are one of the ways our brain stores memory so effectively. If emotions are this powerful in waking life, it stands to reason that they play a critical role in our dreams as well. If all of the other layers of the dream interpretation point to it being psychological in nature, then oftentimes examining the emotions in order from the beginning to the end of the dream will give us a clear answer of what the dream is about. From there you can continue onto steps 5-7 to gain even more insight.

Emotions (provided the dream passes the interpretation worthiness test) are the best tool for determining what triggered the dream. Consider the following dream example:

Imagine you had an early morning releasing dream where you won tickets to a theme park. In the dream you were excited to ride a roller coaster you've always wanted to experience. But when you arrive at the front of the line for your ride, your ticket is not accepted, even though it clearly states that this roller coaster is included. For a moment you are confused, then angry. You yell at the ticket taker. This was the opportunity you had been waiting for, and now you don't get to enjoy it.

Let's examine the emotions of this dream. First there was excitement, then confusion, followed quickly by anger. Where else in your life did you experience this series of emotions in that order? Perhaps it was a new job opportunity that you were so excited for, but a friend who you thought would be excited with you was not, and so you were momentarily confused, and then angry because you believed your friend's enthusiasm would match your own.

The emotions identified in this dream were:

$$\text{Excited} \rightarrow \text{Confused} \rightarrow \text{Angry}$$

Identifying the emotions of your psychological dream is similar to when you finally understand the verb tenses in a new language - something just clicks. And while the understanding of that language may still be rudimentary, you are now able to carry on a conversation between conscious and subconscious.

When identifying the emotions of your dream, go back to the beginning of your recollection of the dream. Oftentimes people will miss that first emotion because it may be subtle (boredom, calm, relaxing, etc), and occurs before the more dramatic parts of the dream. Always include that first emotion. Even though it may not be a triggering emotion, it's important information, as it is likely to be a powerful clue to what your dream is trying to convey.

Don't worry if you're having a hard time pinpointing where else in your life you've experienced the emotions of your dream. There are still three more steps that will help you learn even

Human Dreaming

more about the meaning of your dream. In Chapter 10, I will further break down all seven of the dream interpretation steps and show how the emotions of your dream help to guide you.

Key Takeaways

- Identify the emotions of the dream at the beginning, middle, and end (ex: excited, then confused, then scared)
- Pinpoint where else in your life are you experiencing the emotions from your dream in that particular order
- Review the previously collected clues, and see if they are all pointing in the same direction

Once you understand how emotions guide you within the framework of the dream types (physiological and psychological input), you can begin to tease out the literal and symbolic aspects, thus building upon the next step of your dream interpretation.

Human Dreaming

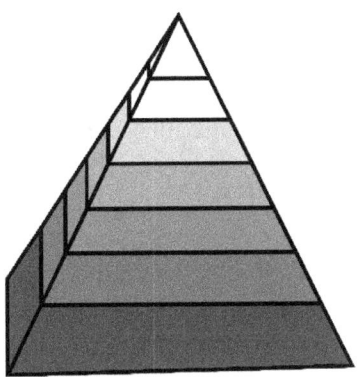

Chapter 7 – Step 5: Symbolic and Literal Aspects

Dreams say what they mean, but they don't say it in daytime language. – Gail Godwin

Consciously, and subconsciously we express ourselves both literally and inferentially to varying degrees. Some of us more frequently express information literally, and some more inferentially, but we all express both sometimes. So, what is our subconscious saying literally, and what parts are inferential or symbolic? Do your dreams skew heavily towards one or the other?

At this stage we start to more fully comprehend the language of Dynamic Dream Interpretation. Once we learn how to separate the literal from the symbolic, we have a much clearer picture of what our subconscious is attempting to say. It's like when we begin to learn our first language, and we might have a few vocabulary words, but once we start to comprehend putting those words together to form sentences, the world just opens up as we see everything through a new lens. With the newly acquired skill of Dynamic Dream Interpretation, the conversations between conscious and subconscious start to have more nuance.

How do you know if the dream is about you, an aspect of your life represented symbolically, or about someone else entirely? More often than not, dream content will at first appear to skew heavily towards the symbolic; but once identified, the literal aspects often carry more information than the symbolic images we see.

Visitors to our dreams in the form of people and animals can be confusing. What appears to be a literal dream about someone else will almost always be a dream about you, and that person or animal is most likely serving in a symbolic capacity. Especially if they are behaving differently than they would in waking life. One notable exception is when we dream about a loved one who has passed away, and we are aware they are deceased in the dream. That may very well be a literal message about that person.

To decipher between literal and symbolic content, ask yourself questions about fundamental aspects of the dream:

- Are you yourself, or someone/something else? If you are yourself in the present or past it points toward the literal.
- If you are someone/something else, you are an older version of yourself, or your current age but the dream is set in the future, that points toward symbolic.

- Check your age. If unsure, it's most likely dealing with present-day you, and will be a literal aspect. If you are younger, the dream is most likely about a literal event that occurred around that age.
- If it's a purely psychological dream, where else in your life are you experiencing the emotions that you identified in the 4th step? These emotions will point to a literal experience.

Answering these questions will allow you to separate the dream content into the literal and symbolic aspects. Consider the sample dream from chapter 6:

> You won tickets to a theme park but were thwarted from taking an exciting opportunity and that made you confused and then angry.

Once you've identified the emotions at the beginning, middle, and end of your dream, think about where else in your life you experienced those emotions (in this example, it was when a friend was unsupportive of your career move), so those emotions and that experience go in the literal category, as follows:

Literal aspects:
- You were you (not someone or something else)
- You were the same age as you are now (not a past or future version of yourself)
- Your dream is processing an experience you had where there was excitement followed by confusion, then anger. In this case, when a thrilling new job opportunity came up but your friend wasn't supportive

Symbolic aspects:

- Winning a ticket might symbolize the exciting job opportunity
- The roller coaster may represent an ambition you've been striving for
- The ticket taker is likely be symbolic of your unsupportive friend since this was trigger for the confusion and anger

The dream may have a lot more content around the visuals and particulars, or the sights, sounds, and stimulus of the theme park, but once broken down, this dream appears to have approximately equal literal and symbolic aspects. The dream type was releasing, and it was psychologically based, with no external physiological factors. Interpreting the emotions as being of importance is the correct course of action.

Most often, psychological dreams will be paired with more current events. But in the rare instances a dream may be dealing with the distant past, or future. Use the following clues to help determine whether these aspects are literal or symbolic:

- I am myself at my current age, but the dream is set far in the future (likely symbolic)
- I am myself, but I am much older than I am right now (likely symbolic)
- I am myself, but I am much younger than I am right now, and I experienced changing emotions from the beginning to the end of the dream (likely literal about the past)

Human Dreaming

- I am myself, set in the present day (if unsure, consider it present day), and experienced changing emotions from the beginning to the end of the dream. (likely literal about recent events)

Now that you're starting to understand the various factors that go into individualized (or dynamic) dream interpretation, you can begin to blend the information provided by each new clue, and uncover new layers of meaning with every step.

If you imagine interpretation as a new language, then the literal aspects are like learning punctuation. A comma here, or an exclamation point there, makes all the difference in understanding messages from the subconscious.

Key Takeaways

- Write down and separate the literal and symbolic aspects of your dream
- Notice how the layers of clues given by the subconscious are stacking up to create a tangible structure
- Identifying the literal aspects will help the dreamer understand the symbology
- By separating the literal and symbolic aspects of your dream, one can begin to glean the fundamental message your subconscious is sending

The next piece of the puzzle is identifying the more subtle clues from your life script. In other words, pinpointing keywords and phrases. Once identified, these will help further clarify what is driving the creation of your dream.

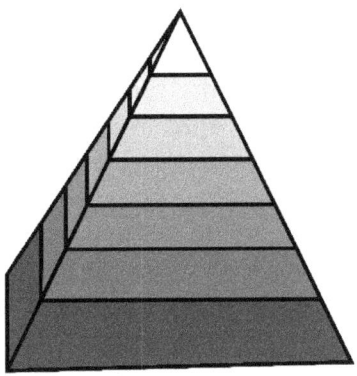

Chapter 8 – Step 6: Keywords and Phrases

Yet, it is in our idleness, in our dreams that the submerged truth sometimes comes to the top.
– *Virginia Woolf*

Keywords and phrases are meaningful expressions that you use to describe the dream, or sometimes quotes that come from the dream itself. Identifying the keywords and phrases is an important step in confirming meaning that was identified in the previous five steps. In this sixth step, review the written dream and see what words or phrases standout in the larger context of what you have already learned about your dream.

It is important to journal your dreams for a few reasons. First, it helps with dream recall. The more often you write your dreams down, the better you are able to remember them. This improved recall applies when you first wake up, as well as remembering details from your dream well into the future. Second, writing triggers the ideomotor response and taps directly into the subconscious life script. This makes journaling your dreams an excellent tool for discovering more literal and symbolic messages from the subconscious. Lastly, keywords and phrases generally only present themselves through writing. When we are examining the dream in our minds, we don't tend to examine the words we use to describe that dream as being important. Writing down your dreams as opposed to examining them only in your mind gives you a much clearer picture of each component, and thus the dream as a whole.

Why am I having this dream now? How could these negative emotions possibly be helpful? What does something from years ago have to do with the present moment? If the meaning of your dream is still escaping you, then this identification step can help to further clarify the origins. Keywords and phrases can be defined as either literal or symbolic, depending on how they fit with the rest of the clues given in the dream. A skilled facilitator can identify most of the keywords and phrases in a written dream, but only the dreamer can accurately identify whether they should be viewed as literal or symbolic.

Observing keywords and phrases is more of an art than a science, and may take some practice before becoming adept at it. Phrases are often easier to identify than keywords since they paint a pretty clear image. Once you see them, it brings an even deeper understanding of your subconscious language. Some examples of common phrases that might be used to describe a seemingly bizarre action in a dream are:

Human Dreaming

- Barking up the wrong tree
- New episode
- Next chapter
- Chip on your shoulder
- Piece of cake
- Beating around the bush
- See eye to eye
- (Once in a) blue moon

Of course, once you see how a common phrase from your culture translates into dream symbology, it can actually look quite literal. For example, if you had a dream that your dog was barking up a tree, but the squirrel was in a different tree, you might use the phrase "barking up the wrong tree" in your written description of the dream. When you look back though all of the aspects of the dream from dream type, to the emotions, etc., it may be literally telling you that you're working towards the wrong job or wrong relationship, and thus "barking up the wrong tree."

Keywords are often descriptive and may be emotionally charged for the dreamer. Some examples might be:

- Survival
- Dying
- Lost
- Found
- Committing
- Fleeing
- Tiny
- Huge
- Important
- Nonchalant
- Ruined
- Fixed
- Guilty
- Innocent

Highlighting these words and phrases is like adjusting binoculars, you could see the image before, but now it becomes more defined. I like to keep various colors of highlighters on hand so I can mark the emotions of the dream in one color, the literal keywords and phrases in another, and the symbolic keywords and phrases in a third color.

In one dream I had, my family and I had to jump out of an airplane into thick clouds and fog with not enough parachutes for everyone. When writing out the dream, I used the phrase, "we took a leap of faith". After going through the steps, I highlighted the keywords and phrases, and that phrase stood out because it confirmed the literal aspects of my dream, as well as the symbolic aspects of skydiving without a parachute.

We had recently downsized from a large house, left full time employment, and our beloved community to adopt a more "location independent" lifestyle to spend more quality time with family. The "leap of faith" phrase not only further clarified what I thought the dream was about, but also confirmed the literal aspect of having recently taken an actual leap of faith into a new lifestyle, and simultaneously illustrated that the symbology of jumping out of the airplane was much closer to literal than I had originally suspected.

Key Takeaways

- Writing down your dreams is the most important step in accurate interpretation
- Consider keeping highlighters on hand so you can highlight keywords and phrases and compare and contrast them to the other aspects of your dream
- Keywords and phrases point directly at the source of the dream

Now that you have learned how to further identify the what, where, when, and why of your dreams, it's time to build a visual representation to provide a comprehensive overview of all aspects of your dream.

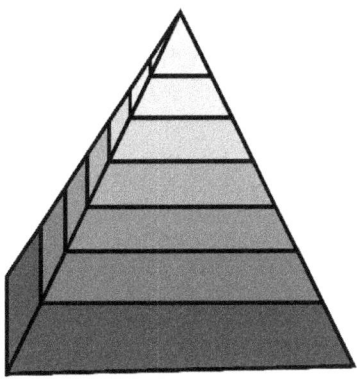

Chapter 9 – Step 7: Visual Overview & Conclusion

I dream of painting, and then I paint my dream.
– Vincent Van Gogh

How to build a visual overview:

Understanding your dreams takes some detective work. But as with any process, the more you practice, the more proficient you become. In time, you will be able to identify the important factors with ease, and learn the meaning of your dream almost immediately. Journaling your dreams and utilizing a visual structure will assist in an even deeper understanding of your subconscious landscape.

You can use the seven step process of dynamic dream interpretation in several different ways. For example, a simple list or pie chart with the first six steps, plus room to write and doodle step 7 underneath it. I use the symbol of a pyramid in my "Human Dreaming" journal because it illustrates a solid foundation, followed by equally important tiers as you build all the way up. You may choose whichever format works best for you.

List:

Dream Content: *Last night I dreamt...*

1. Dream type:
2. Dream subtype:
3. Physiological or psychological:
4. Emotions:
   - Beginning:
   - Middle:
   - End:
5. Literal aspects:
   -
   -
   -

and Symbolic aspects:
   -
   -
   -

6. Keywords and phrases:
   -
   -
   -

7. Visual overview and conclusion:
   -
   -
   -

Human Dreaming

Pie Chart:

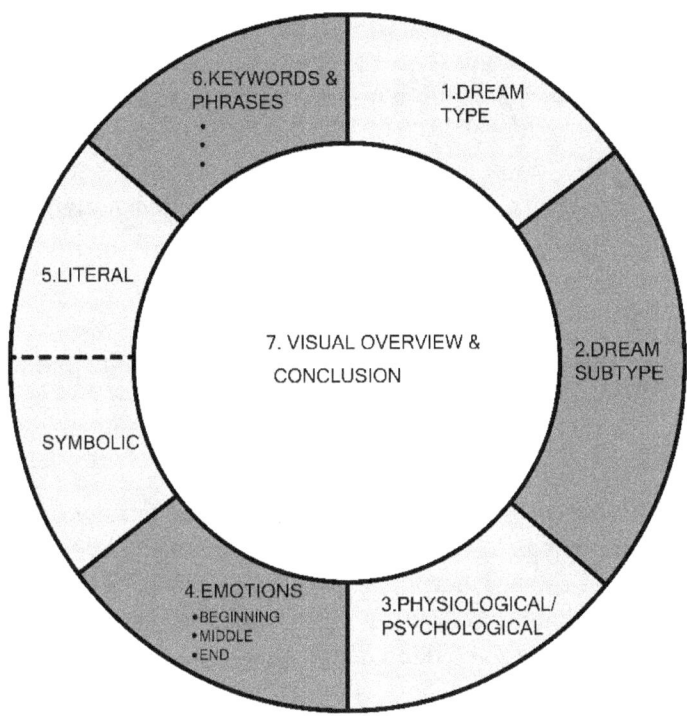

Only you can truly know what the messages from your subconscious mean, so it's important to practice getting to know yourself in a whole new way. Each step provides new insight. Every clue is important. Get familiar with using a visual construct as yet another lens with which to view information from your dream.

With all the tools in hand, and armed with the knowledge of all the various aspects of dreams, you can tie it all together.

Keywords and phrases are bits and pieces of your life script popping from your subconscious and onto paper.
Journaling and/or drawing your dreams will encourage better dream recall. Here are some tips for being able to capture your dreams and stimulate more frequent recollection:

- Drink water before bed at night if you wish to be able to recall more during the predictive dream cycle
- Keep your journal or recorder right next to the bed within easy reach, and write/record your dreams immediately
- Talk to someone about your dreams first thing in the morning

Sample dream overview: Lily had a recurring anxiety dream that continued to worsen until it became a recurring nightmare, causing her to fear going to sleep. The dream became so loud and insistent that it haunted her for over a year, resulting in sleep deprivation, stress, and worry. It was a releasing dream, psychological in nature, and she was herself at her own age, so we knew she was processing something from the present day. Many people from her past appeared in the dream, however, it was the people in her present she dreamed were upset with her.

Her emotions began as neutral but then became increasingly anxious until it would morph into a nightmare about losing her husband, or that her colleagues, professors, or clients were extremely angry with her. When the underlying issues of nightmares - especially recurring ones - are not dealt with right away, the dreamer risks the negative emotions of the dream becoming reinforced instead of let go. In Lily's case the anxiety, fear, and worry were what became reinforced, causing a vicious cycle of insomnia and physical health issues.

After building the first few layers, Lily still wasn't aware of what was causing the nightmares. Once she identified some keywords and phrases, and sketched out her dream on paper, she was finally able to understand what caused the recurring nightmare. She was then able to create a plan to release the emotional baggage associated with the nightmare.

Dream content: I have a recurring nightmare that I am on my college campus and everything is normal until I go upstairs and run into my ex-boyfriend who had rejected me years ago (editing note: he wasn't rejecting her in the dream, he had rejected her years before in real life). Sometimes my former roommate from that time is also there. At this point, I am very anxious and just need some comfort, but when I get to the third floor where my class is, there is always someone very angry and yelling at me. Usually it's my husband yelling that he is leaving me, but sometimes it's a professor, classmate, or client disappointed with my performance. I often wake up crying.

Britt Sheflin

1. Dream type: Releasing/reinforcing
2. Dream subtype: Recurring. Nightmare.
3. Physiological or psychological: Psychological
4. Emotions:
    - Beginning: neutral
    - Middle: anxious
    - End: profound loss/rejection
5. Literal aspects:
    - Self
    - Current age *(indicates present day)*
    - Anxiety
    - Fear of loss/ rejection

and Symbolic aspects:
    - People from the past
    - People from the present
    - Campus setting
    - Anger and yelling

6. Keywords and phrases:
    - Rejected
    - Fear
    - Loss
    - Performance
    - Need some comfort

Human Dreaming

7. Visual overview and conclusion:

This was initially a releasing dream that ended up reinforcing my negative emotions instead of letting them go. Taking steps to address my fear of rejection and communicating my need for comfort are helping greatly.

Once she was able to draw a visual overview with all seven components of the dream next to each other, Lily's dream meaning came into focus. She saw that it was an underlying fear of rejection and loss as she transitioned from college into a new career. Her husband and all of the other people from her present day who were angry at her in her dream, but treated her wonderfully in waking life, were symbolic of her fear of rejection.

Because her rejection had stemmed from a period of time in her life when the people in her past had hurt her, those people appeared as symbols to let her know what period of time the fear of rejection came from. The campus setting was a literal representation of the timing (she'd been a student the entire last year that the dreams were occurring), as well as a symbolic representation of her transition from student to professional.

Lily's dream is more complicated than most. It took until that final step before she was able to see the bigger picture, but by completing all seven steps she finally understood what her dream meant, and was able to get help moving past her fear of rejection.

By drawing a visual overview, the dreamer has another perspective from which to view the dream. The drawings don't need to be pretty, stick figures and line drawings work just fine. This is the final step in the dynamic dream interpretation process; where fluency begins to take place, and all of the grammar, vocabulary, and punctuation of this new language is compiled to form a now readable sentence.

Human Dreaming

When interpreting your dreams, start by writing out your dream. Then, follow the steps below. This will allow you to see all of the layers of your dream in one place.

1. What is the dream type?
2. What is/are the dream subtype(s)?
3. Is it a psychological or physiological dream? (if physiological, you can stop here and examine diet, medications, state of health, or other external factors)
4. What are the emotions present during the beginning, middle, and end of my psychological dream?
5. What are the literal and symbolic aspects?
6. What are the keywords and phrases?
7. Visual overview and conclusion: Sketch your dream. Then looking at all seven components, ask yourself questions. For example: How do all of the layers inform one another? Any keywords and phrases stand out as being literal rather than symbolic? Do the emotions of the dream lead to where all of the other information points?

If you still need further clarity, ask yourself what you might be avoiding. The best way to do Dynamic Dream Interpretation is to use the "Human Dreaming" journal as it is specifically designed for this method. However, you can use any of the methods above (list, chart, pyramid) in a blank journal.

Key Takeaways

- You know yourself better than anyone else. With the right tools, your detective work is going to uncover more useful information than you ever thought possible
- The more you practice your Dynamic Dream Interpretation skills, the faster and easier it is to find meaningful feedback in your dreams
- A visual overview is another great tool for teasing out additional important information

Human Dreaming

Chapter 10 – Examples and Case Studies

Who looks outside, dreams; who looks inside, awakes. – Carl Jung

By writing out and breaking down our dreams into their component parts, we build a window into the deep well of knowledge that is stored in our subconscious, and build the foundation for collaboration between the conscious and subconscious mind.

Understanding communication from the subconscious is part method (breaking down the dream into its component parts), and part intuitive art (looking at all of the clues and painting a meaningful picture).

The following are the questions we ask ourselves in order to break a dream down into its component parts:

- Dream type
    - What portion of my sleep cycle did this dream occur?
    - Sorting, Predictive, or Releasing/Reinforcing?
    - Are there considerations around my recent sleep patterns that may need to be factored in?

- Dream subtype
    - Was it a scary, or happy dream?
    - Is the dream recurring?
    - Is there anything unusual that stands out, such as being in a different time?
- Physiological/Psychological
    - Were there any external factors that might have entered my dream, such as a knock at the door, or a pet climbing into bed?
    - Did the dream have a clear beginning, middle, and end with changing emotions?
    - Are there any substances that may have affected the content of my dreams?
- Emotions
    - What emotions did I experience at the beginning, middle, and end of the dream?
    - Where else in my life have I experienced these emotions in that order?
    - Do these emotions make more sense when viewed through the lens of your dream type, subtype, and physiological/psychological aspects?
- Literal & Symbolic aspects
    - Are you yourself in the dream?
    - Are you your current age?
    - Is the dream set in the present day?
- Keywords and phrases
    - Are there any affecting words that stand out? Affecting words might be ones you use several times, or ones that pertain to the emotions experienced. Some common affecting words are: love, hate, work, home, child, adult, etc.

Human Dreaming

- o Are there any phrases that stand out? These are often cliches from your culture, such as: barking up the wrong tree, standing on shaky ground, the whole hog, etc.
- o Do any of the keywords or phrases stand out as being literal or symbolic? If so, you may add them to those columns.
- Visual overview and conclusion
    - o Draw your dream and see if any new details emerge that help to inform the previous six steps.
    - o With all seven components now in front of you, are you able to see what emotions and experiences the dream is about? What does this information tell you? How can you use this information to help yourself?

In addition to asking ourselves the component questions, we may need to ask ourselves clarifying questions about our waking life, in order to pull everything into focus. Asking the clarifying questions is the more artful part of the process. This is how you come to understand the significance of information that falls outside of the "rules." Honest answers and trusting your intuition will yield good results. Some examples of clarifying questions are:

- Have my sleep cycles been normal recently, or have I been getting too much or too little sleep?
- If my sleep cycles or sleep quality have been disrupted, how might this have affected my dream types?
- What has been going on in my life that might have caused this dream to occur now?

- Have I been consuming any substances that may be intensifying or altering my dreams?
- If my dreams are frequently overly intense, or I'm waking up sweating and shaking, but my blood sugar is stable, what other physiological causes might there be? Have I told my doctor about these symptoms?
- Do my dreams tend to lean more towards the literal or symbolic, and how might knowing that help me understand my dreams?
- How might my personal, cultural, and/or religious beliefs be expressed in my dreams?

The following are real-life examples of Dynamic Dream Interpretation, and dream therapy. The more we can see the whole process in action, the easier it is to apply it to our own dream interpretations. I have recreated the drawings, and edited out any identifying details.

Child Rescue

This releasing dream has both personal elements and collective dreaming elements. Covid-19 dreams are very common right now, because it is an ever-present thought in the collective unconscious in many places around the globe. Depending on where you are and what year it is, collective dreams will vary. They may be about anything occurring globally, or something in your local culture. Personal beliefs also make a strong showing, as the dreamer is from the United States where mask wearing and Covid-19 are highly politicized.

Human Dreaming

Dream content:

A guy friend that was in the group of friends I was hanging out with found two tiny little girls who were lost and hungry. They were skittish and only wanted to be helped by a "mommy" so he had me pick them up. They were so hungry they began suckling my cheeks. They were children I have never seen before in real life, but in the dream, they were so real to me. I even remember their names and faces. "Ginger" said she was 5 but she was the size of a 2-year-old. "Soriayah" was the size of a baby but could talk.

Thinking they were just lost, I got security to help find their parents. When I turned around, I saw a male and female couple and another guy who was with them. They had all three passed out and fallen down some escalators, wasted drunk, and were lying there unconscious. I suddenly realized these girls were severely abused and trying to get away. I wanted to take them home with me. Cops and social services had already been called though, so I couldn't leave with them.

While holding them close, I imagined their futures with me as ballerinas and good, well-adjusted people. Social services came and examined the girls. They said the younger one had a severe hip/leg fracture from abuse. They were still clinging to me when they were taken away. In that short amount of time, I had already become their mom. I was devastated. Shortly afterwards I also realized I had been exposed to Covid-19 because of the irresponsible parents partying in big crowds. I was simultaneously heartbroken and accepting that I had to move forward in the best way I could.

Britt Sheflin

1. Dream type: Releasing (7 am)
2. Dream subtype: Present, collective
3. Physiological/Psychological: Psychological
4. Emotions:
   - Beginning: Normal/fun
   - Middle: Love/Terrified/Optimistic
   - End: Devastated/guilty yet accepting
5. Literal aspects:
   - Self
   - Current age
   - Covid -19

and Symbolic aspects:
   - Irresponsible parents (risky behavior by random people)
   - Lost girls (fragile parents)
   - Suckling from a place of no nutritional value (being together, but not able to touch)
   - Mall (public spaces)
   - Security/cops/social services (representing factors out of the dreamer's control)

6. Keywords and phrases:
   - Followed
   - Abuse
   - Clinging to me
   - Unconscious
   - Get away
   - Move forward

Human Dreaming

7. Visual overview & conclusion:

The dreamer had been recently displaced from their beloved home during a natural disaster and was temporarily staying with her parents who had compromised immune systems. The worry was that she would unwittingly bring home Covid-19 to her parents. They had all been so careful with each other and now they were in close proximity out of necessity, all those fears came out in her dreams. The emotions of the dream matched up perfectly with being at home one day under normal circumstances, and fleeing a hurricane the next. Love, fear, and optimism for her parents were followed by the devastation and acceptance of losing her home and the lingering guilt of having possibly exposed her parents.

Discovering what the meaning was behind the dream allowed her to release the devastating emotions of having let the abused little girls down, and focus on the relationship with her parents. She was simultaneously able to "get away" and "move forward".

Dream Vacation

Reinforcing dreams are not as frequently interpreted as releasing, because most dreamers simply enjoy the pleasant dreams, while they may feel a need to understand or vent out the feelings from bad ones. I like to interpret my own joyful reinforcing dreams, because knowing what is being reinforced helps to enhance the effects. The following dream is a lovely example of experiencing pleasure from the subconscious mind.

Dream content:

My partner and I were renting a vacation home. I don't know where we were geographically. The window was open and a large bird flew into the room and came toward me. It seemed happy to have found me, and climbed right up onto my arm. It was huddling into my body and rubbing its head on me and would not let me put it down. In my dream, I remember thinking that the bird must belong to someone, and was either abandoned or flew away and got lost. I thought that it must be happy to have found people and must be very tired and hungry.

I told my partner that we would have to put out flyers to see if anyone had lost their bird, and that if no one responded, we should keep it. I remember feeling that it was wondrous and exciting to have this beautiful bird come to me, and remember the soft feel of the feathers. I felt a lot of warmth toward the bird, and the feeling of the dream was overall very happy.

1. Dream type: Reinforcing (6 am)
2. Dream subtype: Joyful, present
3. Physiological/Psychological: Psychological
4. Emotions:
    - Beginning: Content
    - Middle: Excited
    - End: Wonder/happiness
5. Literal aspects:
    - Self
    - Current age
    - Present day
    - Contentment
    - Happiness

and Symbolic aspects:
- Vacation house
- Bird
- Soft feathers
- Warmth

6. Keywords and phrases:
    - Happy to have found me
    - Wondrous and exciting
    - Come to me
    - Very happy
    - Would not let me put it down
    - We should keep it
7. Visual overview & conclusion:

The dreamer and their partner had recently finished renovating their home. Both of them were working full-time and raising three children while doing the renovations themselves in their spare time. So these feelings of being happy on vacation, and having wonderful things come to them was very real.

The subconscious was reinforcing the satisfaction of their hard work by dreaming about the rewards and pleasure that follows finishing a large project.

Rooftop Danger

The following dream is both predictive and releasing. Because it occurred at the transition point between predictive and releasing, this dream has elements of two different dream types.

Dream content:

I was with a close group of friends and family watching and doing many activities from a slippery, sloped rooftop with no guard rail. I'm not sure why we were on such a dangerous roof. It was a beautiful sunny day. The kids were playing on these fancy splash pad things in the lake and my friend was hang gliding above us. You could tell it was his first time, but he was doing a pretty good job. Suddenly, he dipped out of view, so almost everyone stood up to get a better look. They quickly saw that he was okay but continued watching too close to the edge.

At the same time, all eyes were taken off the kids in the water. So many things were happening all at once. My mom was standing the closest to the edge and I could see that the person behind her was unsteady. Right as I was starting to warn her, the person behind her lurched forward and knocked her off the roof (presumably to her death). I felt terrible that I couldn't keep her safe and my grief woke me up.

1. Dream type: Predictive with releasing elements (3 am)
2. Dream subtype: Present, nightmare
3. Physiological/Psychological: Psychological
4. Emotions:

- Beginning: Content/fun
- Middle: Worried/cautious
- End: Guilt/grief

5. Literal aspects:
   - Self
   - Current age
   - Present day

and Symbolic aspects:
   - Lake
   - Rooftop
   - Falling to death
   - Hang glider
   - No guard rail
   - Unsteady person
   - Mom

6. Keywords and phrases:
   - No guard rail
   - Unsteady
   - Get a better look
   - Too close to the edge
   - Knocked her off
   - Slippery slope
   - All at once

Human Dreaming

7. Visual overview & conclusion:

The predictive elements occurred in the first two-thirds of the dream, while the releasing elements came into play at the end. The predictive aspects of the dream were being worried about family, and seeing all of the things that are wrong with the scenario, but not being able to do anything about it due to the slippery slope with no guard rail and too many things happening all at once.

The dreamer had family members who were dealing with age-related health issues and was simultaneously experiencing a rocky romantic relationship during a pandemic with simultaneous unprecedented political and civil unrest in the US. This made protecting herself and the people she loved difficult in several different ways. It was unavoidable that unpleasant things were going to happen to her family soon, but there is no way to stop it, and no way of knowing which thing would knock her off first.

The releasing part of the dream comes in at the end when there is grief and guilt. The grief is at the loss of the mother in the dream, and the guilt is the inability to protect her family from the instability (unsteady) of the current day.

Raining Garbage

The following is an example of a releasing dream. This dream interpretation also had a lot of clues that came out in writing via ample keywords and phrases.

Dream content:

There was a weird phenomenon in the sky. A strange pattern that would shrink and expand into different geometric shapes. At first it was fascinating to watch. Then it shrank into a dark, dense ball and "bounced" off of the horizon and back into the sky where it expanded again until it exploded and the beautiful, sunny sky itself fractured into a bunch of harsh shapes that were different layers of intense colors of light outlining the deep black of outer space, or something even darker, like a negative space. These shapes condensed and began raining what looked like huge boulders from the sky.

Mixed in with huge boulders were old, rusty bedframes, toilets, and other heavy, discarded objects. A steady barrage. At first I tried to decide where I could go that would be safe from the attacks from the sky, but then I realized there was nowhere safe to go and it was a waiting game of chance. I felt like I would have better luck on the other side of the road, but I was stuck where I was because it was too late to get out. Everything continued crashing down and the world looked grey and dystopian outside the relatively intact building I was sheltering in.

There was a large window where I could see everything happening; the sky continuing to rain down heavy, rusty junk. I wondered how all of that junk could have been up there and I didn't know about it. I felt foolish for not knowing. By the end I felt a sort of quiet acceptance that life would be forever different and not as vibrant as before but I had to keep moving forward and help others get to safety.

1. Dream type: Releasing (6:30 am)
2. Dream subtype: Present
3. Physiological/Psychological: Psychological
4. Emotions:
    - Beginning: Horrified fascination
    - Middle: Foolish
    - End: Quiet acceptance

5. Literal aspects:
    - Self
    - Current age
    - Present day
    - Dystopian
    - Steady Barrage

and Symbolic aspects:
    - Geometric shapes
    - Raining down rusty junk
    - Sheltering in building
    - Window to the world

6. Keywords and phrases:
    - Weird phenomenon
    - Fractured
    - Negative space
    - Discarded objects
    - Steady barrage
    - Nowhere safe
    - Too late to get out
    - Crashing down
    - Dystopian
    - Window
    - Junk
    - Foolish
    - Quiet acceptance
    - Forever different
    - Moving forward
    - Help others get to safety

Human Dreaming

7. Visual overview & conclusion:

This dream was about the weird phenomenon of current global events and the steady barrage of junk that was seen through the window of the internet. The dreamer was feeling increasingly anxious about a dystopian future where there was nowhere safe to go, because it was too late to get out and the world would be forever different.

The dreamer was able to release some of the anxiety by adopting quiet acceptance that they had limited control over global events and, as the subconscious suggested, by focusing on moving forward and helping others get to safety.

Recurring Nightmare

An acquaintance of mine was having nightly, terrifying, violent nightmares that left him emotionally shaken. He was so afraid to go to sleep that he became a chronic insomniac. Recurring dreams are the subconscious mind's way of shouting for attention. His subconscious was begging him to deal with these emotions that he was actively avoiding during waking hours.

The dreams were symbolically about a recent failed relationship and were characterized by several recurring dreams about death and dying violently, much as the relationship itself had done. The following is one of those dreams. While his dreams were primarily psychological, there was also a physiological component of low blood sugar indicated by him awakening around the same time each night soaked in sweat and in fight/flight mode.

Additionally, since the dreams were causing a chain reaction of sleep deprivation, his dream cycles shifted to earlier in the night. Timing-wise he was having the dreams in the "Predictive" phase, but since night after night he was losing sleep, his brain compensated in order to get in sufficient REM cycles, and shifted his "Releasing and Reinforcing" dream cycle to earlier in the night.

Once he began forgoing sugar and consuming healthy proteins before bed, he was able to reduce the intensity, duration, and frequency of the nightmares enough to be able to understand and consciously process the underlying emotions surrounding the bad breakup. Here's how one of his recurring nightmares breaks down.

Dream content:

I'm walking down a street during a beautiful day with my good friend. Suddenly a young guy with facial tattoos runs up behind my friend and stabs my friend in the back of the neck until he no longer moves. After this bloody mess, the guy stands up and looks at me. Then walks away.

1. Dream type: Predictive Releasing (2 am)
2. Dream subtype: Recurring, nightmare
3. Physiological/Psychological: Psychological with a physiological component
4. Emotions:
    - Beginning: Normal/happy
    - Middle: Scared
    - End: Horrified/panicky and full of guilt
5. Literal aspects:
    - Self
    - Current age
    - Present day

and Symbolic aspects:
- Good friend
- Murder
- Death
- Dying
- Pain

6. Keywords and phrases:
    - Stabs him in the back
    - Looks at me
    - Bloody mess

Human Dreaming

7. Visual overview and conclusion:

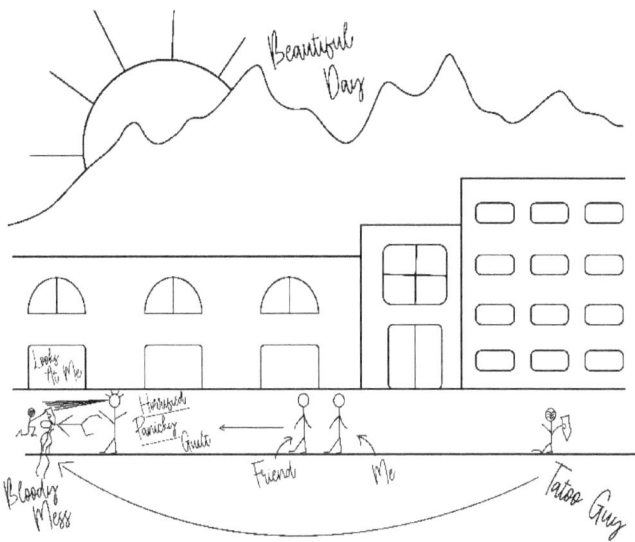

The dreams were about the breakup and how poorly it had gone. I was feeling stabbed in the back, and my life felt like it was a bloody mess.

There was a lot of heartache and pain that hadn't been addressed in a healthy manner, so it was being expressed solely through my dreams.

Once the underlying cause of a recurring nightmare is addressed, it will go away. In this case, managing nutrition in addition to dealing with the emotions of the breakup during waking hours.

The Road Trip

One of my clients was about to embark on a cross country move, while towing a trailer with all of her and her husband's belongings in it. She had plenty of experience driving the trailer, yet she kept having a recurring dream that they would end up wrecked on the side of the road.

As it turns out, her subconscious was aware of something wrong with the trailer brakes that her conscious mind was not aware of, and so the problem kept being presented to her in the predictive phase of dreaming, night after night.

Once she discovered that this was a predictive dream, it caused her to go over the trailer again in even greater detail. She discovered the problem and they were easily able to fix it before they were due to leave. Once the brakes were fixed, the dreams went away and their cross-country journey went smoothly.

Dream content:

I keep having a recurring dream where my husband and I go camping to a beautiful national park. Along the way, we lose control of our camping trailer and it tips over, ruining all of our stuff and leaving us stranded in a remote area.

1. Dream type: Predictive (2:30 am)
2. Dream subtype: Recurring
3. Physiological/Psychological: Psychological

4. Emotions:
    - Beginning: Excited
    - Middle: Scared
    - End: Sad
5. Literal aspects:
    - Self
    - Current age
    - Present day
    - Driving danger
    - Traveling with husband

and Symbolic aspects:
    - Camping
    - Different trailer
6. Keywords and phrases:
    - Along the way
    - Lose control
    - Ruining our stuff
    - Stranded

7. Visual overview and conclusion:

My subconscious had picked up on the danger of the trailer brakes not working properly, even though my conscious mind was not yet aware of any issue with the brakes.

If the dreams had been ignored, perhaps the trailer would have lost control along the way, leaving us stranded, and ruining our stuff. Finding and fixing the problem caused the dreams to stop.

This predictive dream happened to be very literal in nature, but predictive dreams are just as often symbolic in nature. Regardless of the literal or symbolic aspects, if you're fairly certain that your dreams are occurring in the predictive phase, it can be really important to interpret them for your own safety!

New Neighborhood

This another example of a predictive dream, and how your subconscious can tell you what it's ready to change.

Dream content:

In my dream I was riding a motorcycle and I was being followed by a car. It looked like my boyfriend was driving it. I was going around in circles fast. Then cops started chasing me, I kept thinking I had to get away. Before waking up I remember jumping my bike onto a very tall wall. I was looking over the entire city and it was on fire. The police couldn't follow me.

I was about to jump into a new neighborhood, nice houses but no cars. I remember thinking about how I was going to land and realized that my hands were tied behind my back. I woke up before landing at 2:30 am, not scared just normal. No weird sounds, it was actually kind of quiet and nice.

1. Dream type: Predictive (2:30 am)
2. Dream subtype: Present
3. Physiological/Psychological: Psychological
4. Emotions:
   - Beginning: Exciting
   - Middle: Scary
   - End: Relieved to get away from the fire
5. Literal aspects:
   - Self
   - Current age
   - Set in present day
   - Chaos

and Symbolic aspects:
   - Being chased
   - Boyfriend
   - Cops
   - City on fire
   - New neighborhood
   - Very tall wall
   - Hands tied
6. Keywords and phrases:
   - Followed
   - Chased
   - Get away
   - Jumping
   - New

Human Dreaming

- My hands were tied
- How was I going to land

7. Visual overview & conclusion:

This dreamer was going through a very transitional point in life, and had finally learned how to put up some healthy boundaries between her and her chaotic family.

She wasn't sure how she was going to land into this next phase of her life, but she couldn't live the way she had been living before, and thus her hands were tied - she had to get away and create a new pattern.

Understanding that her subconscious mind was ready to have that boundary (wall) set gave her the fortitude needed to maintain those boundaries well into the future.

Recurring Sexual Dream

This dreamer had been having recurring sex dreams with famous actors. They were not necessarily her type in waking life, but were the top "sex symbols" of her generation. She was at an age when many women reach their peak sexuality and their hormones begin to reflect that.

Dream content:

Almost every night I dream that I'm hooking up with Brad Pitt, Idris Elba, Johnny Depp, or some other famous guy, which is weird because I'm not into movies and I definitely don't spend any time pining after them in real life.

In the dreams we just see each other and then are having super-hot sex. I usually wake up just before I climax. Even though I know it's just a dream and I'm not actually cheating on my partner, I always feel a twinge of guilt upon awakening.

1. Dream type: Releasing/reinforcing (5 am - 7 am)
2. Dream subtype: Recurring, sexual
3. Physiological/Psychological: Physiological with a psychological element

4. Emotions:
   - Beginning: Heightened physical arousal
   - Middle: Near or at orgasm
   - End: Guilt upon awakening
5. Literal aspects:
   - Self
   - Current age
   - Set in present day
   - Heightened arousal

and Symbolic aspects:
   - Sex symbol movie stars
6. Keywords and phrases:
   - Super-hot sex
   - Climax
   - Twinge of guilt

7. Visual overview and conclusion:

Hormonal changes are causing heightened arousal. Dreams of having super-hot sex, and awakening before climax .

The twinge of guilt is after awakening, so it's more physiological in nature.

This dream is an illustration of how hormones can play a role in dream types and subtypes. The best clue that this was a physiological experience is that there isn't a clear beginning, middle, or end to the story. The dreamer is simply having sex and is highly aroused by a symbolic stand-In partner. There are

Human Dreaming

no before, during, or after emotions to speak of, just a powerful physical sensation of lust.

The dream is both reinforcing because the highly active hormones are telling the body and subconscious mind that feel-good sex is a really great thing! It's also a releasing dream because there is a little feeling of guilt right at the moment of awakening. Even though she didn't do anything wrong - dream sex is not cheating, after all - the emotions of shame and guilt are being processed due to the dreamer's cultural views on sex.

Ancestor/Spiritual - Sister

I think it was Easter. My friend used to have parties that I went to on Easter. When I walked into the family room my sister (deceased), and my mother (alive), were sitting on the sofa. They were young... Healthy... Happy. I was upset because they didn't tell me they were coming. And I was confused because I knew my sister had passed away.

I can't remember the conversation or what happened after that. But I was relieved to see my sister happy on the other side. Her smile, her body language was happy. I've been thinking about this dream for days. I would like to remember what her and I spoke about.

1. Dream Type: Releasing/reinforcing (6 am)
2. Dream Subtype: Spiritual/ancestor, elements of past
3. Psychological or Physiological: Psychological

4. Emotions:
   - Beginning: Normal/nothing out of the ordinary
   - Middle: Confused/Upset
   - End: Comfort/relieved
5. Literal Aspects:
   - Self
   - Current age
   - Present day
   - Sister deceased
   - Sister younger
   - Mother younger

and Symbolic Aspects:
   - Mom and sister happy and healthy
   - Easter party
   - Friend
6. Keywords and Phrases:
   - Family room
   - Other side
   - Happy
   - Healthy
   - Body language
   - Relieved
   - Remember

7. Visual overview and conclusion:

Processing current life occurrences that are related to a time when the sister and mother were approximately the age they are in the dream.

What event was confusing and upsetting back then, but has led to feeling comfort and relief now?

The dreamer also felt that it might have been an actual visit from her sister letting her know that she is happy and content on the other side.

Britt Sheflin

Spiritual and ancestor dreams have much to do with one's cultural and religious background. For some, these visits from deceased family members are to be perceived literally, and for others it may be interpreted as if all of the people in the dream were still living. Both ways are correct.

Orgasmic Birth

This dream came to me from a friend who had such wonderful experiences during both of her births, she helped me to overcome my pre-programmed fear of childbirth and see that not all childbirth is traumatic. This, along with hypnosis allowed me to have a similarly wonderful experience with childbirth.

Dream content:

When I was younger and about to give birth to my first child, I woke up in the wee hours of the morning, having dreamt that I needed to go have my baby in the forest, surrounded by trees and moss and forest creatures. I was so confident, relaxed, and at peace that I began to feel intense pleasure throughout my whole body. In my dream everything felt so good. I even had an orgasm during labor.

A few weeks later, as my baby was actually being born, I realized that I had released all of my previous fears around giving birth. I just knew, deep inside that my body was strong, healthy, and there was so much pleasure that could be experienced in birth, if I remained open to it.

I was able to imagine myself back in that forest, enjoying every moment of this miracle of life, and in being able to take myself

Human Dreaming

to that memory in my mind, ended up having an orgasmic birth in the clinic also! I felt like my body was built for this, and that I could do anything!

1. Dream type: Predictive Releasing/reinforcing (3-4 am)
2. Dream subtype: Sexual, spiritual
3. Physiological/Psychological: Psychological
4. Emotions:
    - Beginning: Confidence
    - Middle: Relaxation
    - End: Pleasure/ at peace
5. Literal aspects:
    - Self
    - Current age
    - Present day
    - Pregnant
    - Pleasure
    - Orgasm

and Symbolic aspects:
    - Forest
    - Moss
    - Forest creatures

6. Keywords and phrases:
    - Relaxed
    - At peace
    - Confident
    - Orgasm

7. Visual overview & conclusion:

Very literal dream.

It predicted my birth fairly accurately minus the symbolic location.

This is an example of how two dream types can sometimes flow together at the transition points between dream types. The dreamer woke up at the end of the predictive, and the beginning of the releasing/reinforcing phase. She was able to determine this by the timing of the dream, her sudden release of fear around childbirth, and also because she was able to live out a version of her dream in real life. Her subconscious was telling her quite literally what her body was capable of, even though she wasn't consciously aware of the change yet.

Ancestor Visit & Timing Clues

This dream is an example of why it's important to check the timing clues (past, present, future) when identifying the literal and symbolic components of a dream. Note how the dreamer refers to a previous house and car from a previous time.

When we dove a little deeper into the timing clues we discovered that the dreamer was their self at their current age, but the dream was set in the past during a specific period of time. The daughter was also younger than her current age, and the father was the same age he was when the dreamer lived in that house.

These and other clues were discovered by asking the following clarifying questions:

- What age were you in the dream, younger or older than now? Your dad? Your daughter?
- What happened during the period of time you lived in that house and owned that car?
- What was the relationship like between your father and your daughter?
- What was your relationship like with your father?

- Have any emotions or experiences from that time been on your mind recently?

Dream content:

I keep having a recurring dream of my father sitting in the garage, drinking a beer, in a patio chair. It's Spring. I'm washing one of my previous cars, in front of a previous home. My father is overseeing my progress but not saying much. There are buttons in my maple oatmeal; a flavor I won't be eating much longer. I prefer plain. My daughter runs up to me with big energy and clown/harlequin makeup."

1. Dream type: Releasing (5:30 am)
2. Dream subtype: Ancestor, recurring
3. Physiological/Psychological: Psychological
4. Emotions:
    a. Beginning: Content
    b. Middle: Happy to be with my dad
    c. End: Then sad remembering that he had passed
5. Literal aspects:
    - Self
    - Current age
    - Dad, daughter, younger versions of themselves
    - Set in the past

and Symbolic aspects:
- Car
- House
- Maple oatmeal
- Buttons in food
- Harlequin makeup

6. Keywords and phrases:
   - Father is overseeing my progress
   - I prefer plain
   - Big energy

Britt Sheflin

7. Visual overview & conclusion:

The dream was about an event, or events that occurred during the time period(s) depicted in the dream. A younger version of dad and daughter, a previous car and house, and yet the dreamer was still her current age, all point to the period of time the subconscious is dealing with: the time between that house and car and present day.

Having the memories of spending time with her dad gave her feelings of happiness and contentment, yet no longer having her dad around to oversee her progress felt sad. Depending on her spiritual beliefs, it may also mean that she feels her dad is still watching over her.

Whether the dad was actually visiting, or the subconscious was producing his image, these visits were cathartic to the dreamer. This is what was needed - to spend a little more time as a family and know in some sense the father was "overseeing her progress."

The dreamer had not been able to spend as much time with her parents as she had wanted to, and there was some underlying sadness at having lost that time together. Her current self was saddened by that lost time from the past, but by remembering and dreaming of spending this quality time together as a family, the sadness was able to be processed in the subconscious.

Partial Interpretations

Sometimes we have intricate dreams, remembered in vivid detail. Other times, we may awaken to our dreams slipping away, left only with a vague sense that it felt important. In some cases we need to ask all of the component questions plus the additional clarifying questions in order to understand what is being communicated. In other cases, the dreams are so straightforward we might not even need to complete all of the component parts before we understand the meaning of the dream and can decide what to do with the information it presents. The following dreams are examples of how partial dreams may be interpreted.

Britt Sheflin

Chocolate wonderland

Upon waking, my daughter will often tell me about her dreams. Recently she had a dream where "everything was made of chocolate" and she was "tasting everything, and it was fun". She had been going around in the dream and tasting everything. It was basically her version of heaven. This is a great example of a reinforcing dream. Joyful, fun, and nothing dramatic, just pure enjoyment. I wrote down the dream as she described it and then asked her follow-up questions to get her interpretation.

In this case "chocolate" was put under the literal category, as she had just discovered chocolate and her subconscious mind was reinforcing that actual chocolate was something to be regarded as safe and pleasurable. Everything being made of chocolate was symbolic, but the chocolate itself was literal.

Dream content:

Everything was made of chocolate, and I was tasting everything around me, and it was fun.

1. Dream type: Reinforcing
2. Dream subtype: Joyful
3. Physiological/Psychological: Psychological

4. Emotions:
   - Beginning: Wonder
   - Middle: Joy
   - End: Fun
5. Literal aspects:
   - Self
   - Current age
   - Present day, same age
   - Chocolate tasting good

   and Symbolic aspects:
   - Everything made of chocolate
6. Keywords and phrases:
   - Tasting everything around me
7. Visual overview: unnecessary

Conclusion: She was reinforcing a new experience as being fundamentally positive.

Running in Place

By the time we are adults, we've probably all experienced this type of nightmare at one point or another. You're trying to run away from something scary, but it's like running in molasses. You can't move, and it feels like the bad guy is perpetually about to "get" you. Sometimes this dream might manifest in other ways, such as teeth falling out, or falling off of a cliff, but the common thread is that there is no clear storyline, no changing emotions, and no end to the dream besides waking up in fight/flight mode.

This dream clearly illustrates how to decipher between a psychological and physiological dream. Notice how there is no clear beginning, middle, or end, and the dreamer awakens in fight/flight mode, soaked in sweat. In this case all three indicators of having a low blood sugar dream (no clear story, fight/flight mode, and soaked in sweat/shaking) are present. Therefore, the dream does not need to be processed beyond step 3.

Dream content:

I wake up every night soaked in sweat, deeply afraid, and unable to shake the terror I had just been experiencing. All of the dreams are pretty much the same each night. I find myself running away from something or someone on pathways in the forest or sometimes on suspended bridges. I can't ever seem to get ahead, and everything around me is strangely blurry. I try to yell for help, but nobody ever comes.

1. Dream type: Predictive (2 am)
2. Dream subtype: Nightmare, recurring
3. Physiological/Psychological: Physiological
4. Emotions: N/A
5. Literal aspects: N/A
    and Symbolic aspects: N/A
6. Keywords and phrases: N/A
7. Visual overview: N/A

Conclusion: The dream was physiologically based. No valid psychological meaning is present.

Once the dreamer has identified this type of recurring physiologically based nightmare, it becomes much easier to release the fear, and also to make sure that steps are taken to stabilize blood sugar while sleeping, by avoiding sugars and consuming high quality proteins before bed.

If your blood sugar is stable and these types of nightmares continue to occur, it may be a symbol of some other health issue, and should be brought to the attention of your doctor as soon as possible.

Dream Therapy for Stopping Cigarettes

On the one year anniversary of her quitting, a stop smoking client of mine had a "brief, yet extremely upsetting dream where I began smoking again." During her waking time, she had no desire to smoke. Given it was the one year anniversary of when she quit, it made sense that she would have a releasing/reinforcing dream about stopping smoking. Her subconscious was processing the feelings of disgust and disappointment that drove her to quit smoking in the first place.

Together, we were able to interpret the dream, despite it being only the one sentence description. From the interpretation of that brief sentence, I created a guided imagery session to help reinforce the positive new habits she had developed. The negative feelings from the dream were quickly processed, and she was able to resume normal life feeling confident in her ability to continue living a smoke-free life.

Britt Sheflin

Dream content:

I had a brief, yet extremely upsetting dream where I began smoking again.

1. Dream type: Releasing/reinforcing (5 am)
2. Dream subtype: Failure/anxiety
3. Physiological/Psychological: Psychological
4. Emotions:
   - Beginning: Horrible
   - Middle: Upsetting
   - End: Disappointing
5. Literal aspects:
   - Self
   - Current age
   - Set in present day
   - Negative feelings towards smoking

   and Symbolic aspects:
   - Starting to smoke again
6. Keywords and phrases:
   - Upsetting
   - Smoking again
7. Visual overview: Unnecessary

Conclusion: The subconscious was still in the process of releasing the desire to smoke, and reinforcing that smoking again would be an upsetting and disappointing thing to do. The subconscious associations are now in alignment with the conscious desire to remain smoke-free.

Stolen Baby

This dream was brought to me for analysis so that the emotions of the dream could be brought down, and not affect this young single mom while she was trying to function at her high-pressure career.

She had briefly dated a colleague who was "too perfect, too quickly" and it set off a series of red flags in her subconscious that later proved to be well-founded. The dream occurred shortly after she broke off both the professional and romantic relationship.

Dream content:

I had a newborn who was stolen. I spent the dream trying to find the baby and running away from whomever else was coming after me. I don't remember much else.

1. Dream type: Releasing (4 am)
2. Dream subtype: Nightmare, recurring (once only)
3. Physiological/Psychological: Psychological
4. Emotions:
    - Beginning: Normal
    - Middle: Fear
    - End: Determination
5. Literal aspects:
    - Self
    - Current age
    - Present day
 and Symbolic aspects:
    - Stolen newborn

6. Keywords and phrases:
   - Newborn
   - Stolen
   - Running away from
7. Visual overview: unnecessary

Conclusion: The dreamer was releasing the emotions surrounding the new(born) relationship, letting go of what had been stolen from her, and running away from a dangerous scenario.

Abuse Nightmare

This dream illustrates that other people in our dreams often serve as symbols and are not automatically literally themselves. In this case, the dream was had by a young teen girl who had a sudden growth spurt over summer break, and was starting to be noticed in a new way by her peers and the adults around her. Her body was changing, and so was her place in the society. She had been going through a mourning process of missing childhood, and was worried about what her role as a grown up would be.

Dream content:

I dreamt my dad severely abused me, even though he has never been anything but an amazing father.

The dream was so vividly awful and scary that I couldn't even look at him for the next two days, and I find I'm still unable to talk to him for more than a minute or two. We've always been very close, and I'm afraid that this dream will ruin our relationship. I just want to go back to the way we were before.

1. Dream type: Releasing (7 am)
2. Dream subtype: Nightmare, present
3. Physiological/Psychological: Psychological
4. Emotions:
   - Beginning: Discomfort
   - Middle: Fear
   - End: Sadness
5. Literal aspects:
   - Self
   - Current age
   - Present day

   and Symbolic aspects:
   - Dad
   - Abuse
6. Keywords and phrases:
   - Severely abused
7. Visual overview: unnecessary

Conclusion: The father in the dream was symbolic of all of the other people in a position of power over her that were suddenly treating her differently. Her subconscious was wary of the new kind of attention she was receiving, which led to the discomfort, fear, and sadness that she experienced both in the dream and in waking life. While she wasn't worried about any one person specifically abusing her, her subconscious was associating the physical changes as a new type of danger.

Britt Sheflin

Serial Killer Escape

Dream content:

I made a plan to escape from a serial killer and trap them inside a warehouse, but every time I tried to get my kid in the car or buckled in, she either wandered away or wouldn't follow instructions, no matter how much I begged or yelled. I was finally able to get her in and away even though my plan was sprung very late.

1. Dream type: Releasing (8 am)
2. Dream subtype: Present
3. Physiological/Psychological:
4. Emotions:
    - Beginning: Worried/concerned
    - Middle: Panicky/frightened and also confused
    - End: Relieved but still anxious
5. Literal aspects:
    - Self
    - Current age

and Symbolic aspects:
    - Uncooperative child
    - Serial killer
6. Keywords and phrases:
    - Plan to escape
    - But every time I tried…
    - No matter how much I begged or yelled
    - My plan was sprung very late
7. Visual overview: Unnecessary

Human Dreaming

Conclusion: This was a releasing dream about political and civil unrest in the dreamer's country of origin. The uncooperative child was symbolic of fellow citizens not seeing the impending danger the serial killer (governmental regime) was posing to the populace.

The original plan (to escape) had been to be traveling out of the country for 6 months of every year, but now that the political situation was more dangerous by the day, the consideration for complete expatriation was much stronger. Unfortunately, moving to another country during a pandemic delayed all travel and thus the plan was sprung very late.

Walk the Plank

We don't often get insight into sorting dreams. Partially because they occur at the beginning of our REM cycle when the brain is still sorting information and building coherent storylines out of our subconscious symbology, and partially because we don't generally wake up until we've entered the predictive phase, if not the releasing/reinforcing phase. Sorting dreams don't typically have a coherent storyline, and may be a mishmash of various symbology.

The closest I got to getting a view into a sorting dream, was after I fell asleep on a couch and about 45 minutes into sleep, I was heard saying, "Well, someone is about to walk the plank!". I have no recollection of this dream, but I believe it had something to do with the pandemic.

For obvious reasons, I was not able to get a complete interpretation, but even with these few clues, I was able to learn some things. Here is what I gathered from the dream:

Dream content:

Walk the plank!

1. Dream type: Sorting, possibly predictive given recent restless sleep cycles (11 pm)
2. Dream subtype: unknown
3. Physiological/Psychological: Psychological
4. Emotions:
    - Unknown
5. Literal aspects:
    - Unknown

   and Symbolic aspects:
    - Walk the plank
6. Keywords and phrases:
    - Walk the plank
    - Someone
7. Visual overview: Unnecessary

Conclusion: None

Again, it is not common to interpret sorting dreams, for a few reasons.

a) Unless we are woken up during that sleep cycle, it's highly unlikely that any dreams in this cycle will be recalled.

Human Dreaming

b) We're not usually in our deeper REM cycles during the sorting phase, which is where the more coherent dreams with actual storylines occur.
c) Much of the information that is processed during this phase is not going to be kept in our long-term memory, so any information contained therein is not likely to be as important as what is presented to us during the predictive and releasing/reinforcing dream stages.

There is an aspect of artistic creativity to deciphering your dreams. The component and clarifying questions and visual overview are the tools with which you break the dream down. Once you have all of these separate parts, it's up to you to figure out how they go back together in such a way that provides meaningful information.

There is no one right way to do this, but by now you should have all of the skills available to see your dreams for the masterpieces they are. And like all of the best art, the more you examine your dreams the more layers of meaning you will discover.

Key Takeaways

- By observing examples of other people's dreams, you can learn more about how your own subconscious symbology presents itself
- A wonderful learning tool is to help interpret the dreams of your friends and family. It's a great way to step outside of your own dream reality, and see the process through a new lens
- Remember that you cannot tell others what their symbology means, but you can guide them through the components, help them ask clarifying questions, and offer up new perspectives

Once you have mastered deciphering your own subconscious symbology and helped others to do the same, you can begin to create a conscious dialogue and create lasting change within your subconscious mind.

Chapter 11 Mental Cinema

Saddle your dreams before you ride 'em.
– *Mary Webb*

Now that you can better understand messages from your subconscious, you may want to learn how to communicate back to it. Learning how to communicate back to the subconscious allows you to do two things:

1. Take the information from a dream, and process the emotions of that dream in a healthy manner.
2. Reprogram your subconscious and make behavior modifications that allow you to live a better future.

We tend to think of thoughts as ephemeral things - here one moment and gone the next - but in reality, every thought we think travels along a tangible and physical neural pathway. The more often we think the same thought, the stronger and more active that pathway becomes. Thoughts in the form of our inner dialogue, or life script, feelings, and automatic behaviors (habits), are like superhighways in the brain - Wide open, and set for the fastest/easiest route to take. Shrinking those superhighways that no longer serve you, while building up the ones that take you to a better life experience may take some work, however the reward is much greater than the effort.

Consciously directing your daydreams can accelerate desired change by physically building new neural pathways in the brain. In Chapter 2 we discussed what our life script is, and how it affects our daily and dream lives. In the following chapters we learned to listen to the language spoken by the subconscious. In this final chapter we will introduce some methods for communicating desired changes back to the subconscious.

The subconscious mind only makes changes when that change will produce greater pleasure, or create a new sense of safety. So, the most effective habit changes occur when the subconscious mind is in agreement with conscious desires, and are perceived as a net benefit. I often share the phrase, "let's imagine a better future together!", with my clients to introduce how hypnosis helps to alter subconscious programming. The following exercises allow you to imagine a better future on your own, with both your conscious and subconscious focused on the same goal. All three techniques help to create new neural pathways that accelerate desired change. You may utilize any or all of them to enhance your waking dreams, which will in turn be reinforced in your sleeping dreams.

OMMM (One Minute Mindfulness Meditation)

This is a wonderful tool for getting your subconscious mind on board with helping you achieve a consciously desired goal. I like to share this technique with all of my clients. Follow the instructions below for creating your personalized imagery, and then either record an audio version on your phone, listening to the OMMM recording every day, or until you are easily able to do the visualization just in your mind with a 60-90 second timer.

Step 1. Draw a picture of yourself (Stick figures and simple line drawings are great!) doing something representative of having achieved your goal. Examples might include: crossing the finishing line at the Boston Marathon, having a celebratory lunch with coworkers due to a promotion, or going on a shopping spree because you have reached your fitness goals. Include a lot of rich detail, such as the time of day, noting the temperature, what you are wearing, who is there, etc.

Step 2. Attach all 5 senses *and one exalted emotion* to your imagery. Write them down on the side of your drawing. For example:

> I **see** the finishing tape, and my family smiling in the crowd.
> I **hear** the people in the crowd cheering me on.
> I can **taste** the Gatorade from the last hydration station.
> I can **feel** my muscles get a last-minute burst of energy, and the breeze on my face.
> I can **smell** the sweat beading on everyone's skin.
> I am **experiencing** the exalted emotion of pride at having achieved my goal of running the Boston Marathon.

Step 3. Keep this drawing with you until you can memorize all the details from your drawing and the sensations and emotions that accompany it. It should feel really good! If something feels unpleasant, adjust the imagery until it feels great.

Step 4. Create your own 60-90 second audio recording describing your imagery, or use the free recording on my website **www.brittsheflin.com/free-resources**. While listening to your recording, powerfully visualize, as if it were happening in the present moment. If you can't see images in your mind, that's perfectly okay, just try to get a sense of what it is like to have this wonderful experience of achieving your goal. If stray thoughts enter, kindly thank them and ask them to come back later, because you're doing important work right now.

Step 5. Repeat, repeat, repeat! Repetition is key to changing your subconscious thought patterns. I recommend doing your visualization at least once per day for a minimum of two months for simple changes. Practice longer for more complicated changes. Some good times to practice the OMMM exercise are: first thing in the morning, last thing at night, or anytime you have one minute alone (such as in the bathroom, or when you park your car before going in to work).

3-5 Minute Self-Hypnosis

Much like meditation, an effective self-hypnosis practice does not require hours every day. Short amounts of focus can produce excellent results! If you already have a meditation practice, you will still benefit from adding self-hypnosis to your routine. Meditation is wonderful for releasing, processing emotions, and changing perception.

Self-hypnosis is great for creating meaningful change in habits and behaviors, as well as allowing you to feel good about yourself in the present by imagining a better future. When we actively imagine ourselves experiencing new opportunities in self-hypnosis, we build new thought patterns that encourage our subconscious minds to allow for positive change through a combination of breath, imagination, and relaxation.

Human Dreaming

The following instructions for creating a short but powerful self-hypnosis practice can be done alone or combined with your existing mindfulness or meditation practice. The subconscious mind is most receptive during the first 30 minutes after waking and the 30 minutes before falling asleep, so these are excellent times to add a self-hypnosis practice to your schedule.

Find a comfortable place to sit and close your eyes. Take three slow, deep belly breaths, feeling your chest and belly expand and contract with each breath. Try to make the exhales last for twice as long as the inhales.

Allow your breathing to return to its natural rhythm, bring your focus to your eyelids. Relax them. After a couple of breaths, relax them again twice as much. And twice as much again.

Bring your attention to your jaws. Relax them... Relax them again twice as much... And twice as much again.

Bring your attention to your shoulders. Relax them... Relax them again twice as much... And twice as much again.

Imagine your favorite place in nature. Bring in all 5 senses here. Observe the sights, sounds, aromas, sensations, and tastes of this place.

Counting backwards slowly from 5 to 0, in time with your breath, say to yourself each number on the inhale, and "calm", "serenity", or another word that feels good to you on the exhale. When you get to "0" say to yourself "deep relaxation" on the exhale.

For example:

> Inhale: 5
> Exhale: calm
> Inhale: 4
> Exhale: calm
> Inhale: 3
> Exhale: calm
> Inhale 2:
> Exhale: calm
> Inhale: 1
> Exhale: calm
> Inhale: 0
> Exhale: Deep Relaxation

Once you have achieved relaxation you can begin to imagine your future self. You may choose to see yourself in whatever way feels best - in a crystal ball, on a movie screen, or perhaps in a magical mirror.

Observe your future self having achieved your goals and feeling so happy about it. Picture yourself switching places with that future you. Notice how good it feels to be there!

What does this achievement sound like, feel like, and look like? Think back to all the steps you took to get there and the new thought patterns you built along the way.

Allow yourself to go forward in time even more and see what good things continue to happen. For example, if you have a fitness goal, vividly imagine yourself reaching your goal weight or size and all the wonderful feelings that come with this success.

Then continue moving forward in time and seeing all of the wonderful benefits that have rippled through your life as a result of the changes you made. Say to yourself several times, "This feels so good, and I deserve it".

Count yourself up and out with your last 5 breaths:

1. Sealing the door to my subconscious mind
2. Bringing with me all positive benefits and learnings
3. Drawing my awareness back into the room
4. Feeling good in my body
5. Eyes open and alert

Dream Journaling

Dream journaling is done first thing in the morning, so be sure to keep your journal and writing implement within arm's reach. Before you even get out of bed, while the dream is still vivid, begin writing the dream down in as much detail as desired.

Once the dream has been written down, you can break the dream down into its component parts right away, or you may choose to come back to the dream interpretation a little later, like while sipping your morning tea.

The most important part when beginning to dream journal, is to enhance your dream recall by getting it onto paper as quickly as possible. Once the dream has been written down, there's no rush to interpret it right away.

For example, you might wake up having had a dream about swimming with narwhals. If you don't write it down right away, you might remember that you had a dream about narwhals, but you would likely forget all of the other vivid details such as the breaching whales, cuddly otters, and seabirds swooping overhead, not to mention the all-important emotions of the dream.

Once you have your dream broken down into its component parts, then you can begin examining the messages contained within. Those messages from the subconscious can then be used in multiple ways. You can use them to help properly process stuck emotions simply by recognizing the dream type, what is being symbolized, and identifying what part of your life those emotions sprang from. You can use the information from your dream in therapy to help accelerate processing of what is important in your life right then. You might even identify a physiological aspect that points to needing medical intervention.

While these techniques are very effective with practice and consistency, some people prefer to create change with the assistance of skilled practitioners. If DIY techniques are not for you, try working with a psychologist, hypnotherapist, or both. Psychology paired with hypnotherapy at the same time creates the most rapid transformations.

Within the pages of this book, you have everything you need to not only interpret the messages coming from the subconscious mind, but also the tools to communicate conscious desires back to the subconscious. Just like learning a new language, it takes consistent, long-term practice. But once this dialogue in a new language "clicks", that communication will become second nature, just like having a conversation in your native language.

Britt Sheflin

A Parting Thought

We can't erase history, but we can overwhelm it with the future – Unknown

I hope that you have found this book to be helpful in deciphering the clues that your subconscious mind delivers to you on a nightly basis. My wish is that it enables you to create a healthy dialogue with your subconscious, and allows you a greater ability to release unwanted thoughts, feelings, and programming, while also being able to reinforce new positive associations and learnings.

I welcome you to join the Human Dreaming community on Facebook and Instagram. You can also subscribe to the Human Dreaming podcast about all things dreamy.

Happy dreaming, Britt

Britt Sheflin

Acknowledgements

First and foremost, I would like to thank Connie Berg of Sunshine Press. From half a world away she gave me a chance, and breathed life into a book that may have otherwise languished on my laptop. Her tireless efforts on behalf of readers of this book are damn near heroic.

I am indebted to the late Dr. John Kappas, who shared his brilliant Dream Therapy techniques with generations of students. Thanks also to George Kappas, who taught me his father's techniques. It was George's Dream Therapy course that reignited my immense curiosity about dreams, and left me with a long list of questions that I was determined to find the answers to. I began studying, sorting, and analyzing thousands of dreams, and with each dream new questions and answers arose. Each new answer informed how I interpreted subsequent dreams and it led me to create Human Dreaming, first as a guide for myself and later as a book that I hope anyone who is curious about dreams will find useful.

Kudos to Daniel Brenner IV, for having the patience of a saint while reading everything that I (a non-writer) jot down in an incoherent jumble. From the benefits of beaver reintroduction to the meaning of dreams, he has helped my mediocre writing become impactful, with little to no benefit to himself.

Thank you to Conan, for so many things in life, but mostly for your shenanigans that included the divine intervention of bringing home the young hitchhiker (one of many), Selah Raines, so many years ago. She's been a steadfast friend, fierce protector, and sage advisor since that first moment.

Britt Sheflin

Marissa Lee Harris who is far more intelligent and educated than I, yet still seeks my advice, deserves more thanks than I could give. She shares generously from her wealth of knowledge, and I wouldn't be who I am today without her guidance and fast friendship.

Profound thanks to Betty and Howard Greager, for allowing me the gift of writing this book in their beautiful mountain home, where many a non-fiction book, and 3 generations of family grew and thrived.

Finally, my enduring gratitude to Liz, Hollis, Monet, Lindsey, Tamara, Cheri, Stephanie, Fred, and all the rest of the wonderful dreamers in my life who have allowed me into their subconscious worlds. Your support and encouragement with every endeavour continues to fuel my fire.

Human Dreaming

Sometimes dreams are wiser than waking. - *Black Elk*

Britt Sheflin C.Ht. is a Certified Hypnotherapist, proud member of the Hypnotherapists Union Local 472, honors graduate of HMI College of Hypnotherapy, and advocate of the importance of dreams. When not dreaming, Britt can be found assisting her clients through dream therapy, or hiking in the mountains with her family.

Britt Sheflin

www.ingramcontent.com/pod-product-compliance
Lightning Source LLC
Chambersburg PA
CBHW070257010526
44107CB00056B/2486